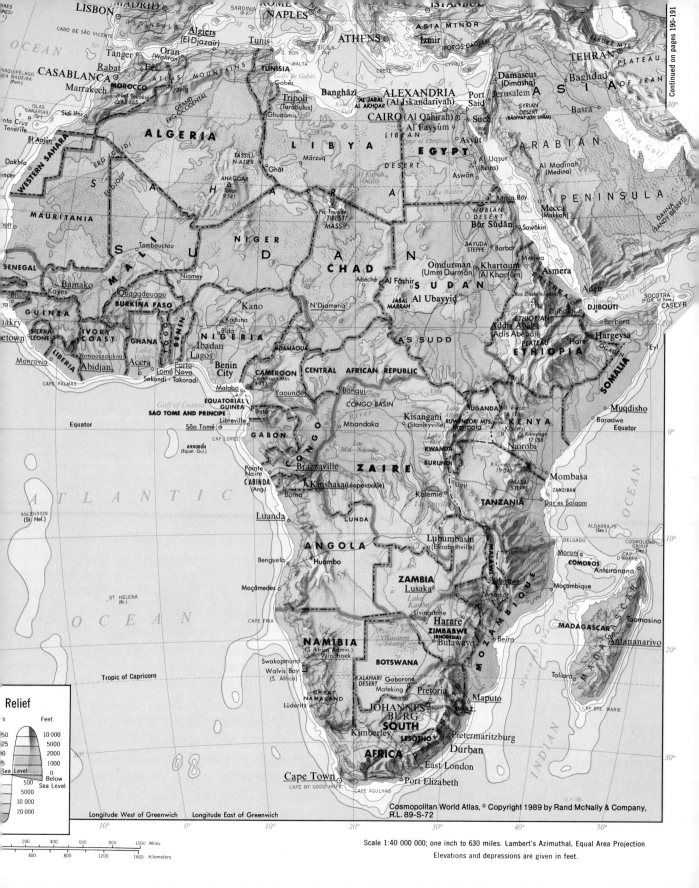

Enchantment of the World

ZAMBIA

By Jason Lauré

Consultant for Zambia: John Rowe, Ph.D., African Studies Faculty, Northwestern University, Evanston, Illinois

Consultant for Reading: Robert L. Hillerich, Ph.D., Bowling Green State University, Bowling Green, Ohio

CHILDRENS PRESS®
CHICAGO

Young girl in a village cooking fish

Library of Congress Cataloging-in-Publication Data

Lauré, Jason.
    Zambia / by Jason Lauré.
        p.   cm. — (Enchantment of the world)
    Includes index.
    Summary: Introduces the geography, climate, history,
people, industry, and culture of Zambia.
    ISBN 0-516-02716-6
    1. Zambia—Juvenile literature.   [1. Zambia.]
I. Title. II. Series.
DT963.L36 1989   89-34281
968.94—dc20   CIP
                                                          AC

Picture Acknowledgments
AP/Wide World Photos, Inc.: 40, 43 (2 photos), 50
The Granger Collection, New York: 12, 14 (2 photos), 15,
16 (2 photos), 28, 101 (top left)
Historical Pictures Service, Chicago: 18, 21, 27, 30 (left)
Journalism Services: © Fotex/König/Sro: 51
© **Jason Lauré:** 5, 8, 34, 47, 52, 53, 54, 55, 60 (2 photos), 63,
64, 67 (right), 68 (middle & right), 75, 77 (left), 78, 85
(right), 87 (left), 93, 95 (2 photos), 99, 111, 113 (right)
© **Ian Murphy:** 59, 73 (left), 84, 88 (4 photos), 98 (left), 101
(right), 106, 108
North Wind Picture Archives: 24, 30 (right)
Photri: 9, 10, 96, 98 (right), 101 (middle), 102
Root Resources: © Jane P. Downton: 100 (left); © Irene
Hubbell: 100 (right)
Shostal Associates: Cover, 86, 94 (left)
Tony Stone Worldwide: 6, 94 (right), 104; © Ian Murphy:
4, 67 (left), 68 (left), 73 (right), 74 (left), 82, 85 (left), 92; ©
David Higgs: 83
Valan: © Joyce Photographics: 74 (right); © Denis Roy: 77
(top right); © Harold V. Green: 77 (bottom right);
© Stephen J. Krasemann: 87 (right); © Christine Osborne:
113 (left)
Zambia National Tourist Board: 101 (bottom left)
Len W. Meents: Maps on 86, 94, 96
**Courtesy Flag Research Center, Winchester,
Massachusetts 01890:** Flag on back cover
Cover: Kariba Dam on the Zambezi River

Women carry sugarcane to market

TABLE OF CONTENTS

Chapter 1

IN THE HEART OF AFRICA

Zambia is a butterfly-shaped country nestled in the very heart of the African continent. It covers 290,586 square miles (752,614 square kilometers), making it about one-tenth larger than the state of Texas or slightly smaller than the nation of Turkey. Landlocked in south-central Africa, Zambia borders on eight countries. It is more than 600 miles (966 kilometers) from the Atlantic Ocean to the west and 500 miles (805 kilometers) from the Indian Ocean to the east. Its capital city, Lusaka, is more than 800 miles (1,287 kilometers) south of the equator.

ZAMBIA'S NEIGHBORS

Zambia shares its longest border with Zaire, to the north. Zaire's Shaba Province juts into Zambia, emphasizing the division between the country's east and west halves. The Luapula River and Lake Mweru form a large part of this border with Zaire. On the northeast is Tanzania and Lake Tanganyika forms part of this border. To the east lies Malawi. On the southeast is Mozambique. The southern border is formed by a 500-mile (805-kilometer)

Opposite page: Zambians make handsome basketwork for everyday use.

The Zambezi River forms part of the southern border.

stretch of the Zambezi River, which separates Zambia from
Namibia, Botswana, and Zimbabwe. Lake Kariba also forms a
large part of the border with Zimbabwe. To the west and
northwest lies Angola.

This complicated location, with so many neighbors crowding
around it, forms not only Zambia's physical shape, but also much
of its current political and economic climate. Zambia's relations
with these eight countries range from complete cooperation to
antagonism. Southern Africa continues to exist in a state of
turmoil, with struggles for political control a decades-long reality.
These hostilities force people from their lands, many fleeing across
the various borders into Zambia. The country's president,

Victoria Falls, with Zambia on the left and Zimbabwe on the right

Kenneth Kaunda, has made it well known that Zambia will receive them willingly. This puts a great economic burden on Zambia and its people. It also increases the tensions between the governments of these countries.

GEOGRAPHY AND CLIMATE

Much of Zambia is a plateau lying at a comfortable altitude, between about 2,700 and 4,500 feet (823 and 1,372 meters). A highlands area stretches toward Tanzania, while the Mafingi Mountains lie along the eastern border with Malawi. There are two lowland areas—in the east is the Luangwa River valley and in the south, the Zambezi River valley. Much of the country enjoys a pleasant climate, with the seasonal changes marked more by rainfall than by extremes of temperature. About 70 percent of the country is covered by Miombo woodland, a mix of shrubs, trees, and tall grasses. Zambia's principal mineral resource is copper. Smaller amounts of other minerals also are found there, including gold, silver, and emeralds. The country also has large coal deposits.

The driest parts of Zambia are the southern and low-lying eastern areas.

Zambia has three fairly distinct seasons: cool and dry from April to August; hot and dry from August through about October; and warm and rainy from about October through March or April. But rainfall amounts vary within the country, with the heaviest rainfall occurring in the northern portions of the two "wings" of the butterfly. This makes some areas unsuitable for farming without irrigation. The driest parts of the country are the southern and low-lying eastern areas. This area is sometimes hit by drought. Although Zambia does have many natural lakes and rivers, the land often suffers from either too little or too much water at different times of the year.

Zambia is divided into eight provinces. Northwestern, Western, Southern, Copperbelt, and Central form the western wing of the nation, while the eastern wing is made up of the Eastern, Northern, and Luapula provinces. In 1976, Lusaka and its surrounding area was designed as the ninth province.

Chapter 2

A LAND OF MANY
DIFFERENT PEOPLE

ANCIENT ZAMBIANS

Stone tools found in Zambia's river valleys show that people lived in the territory some 200,000 years ago. At least 100,000 years ago, a thriving community existed around Kalambo Falls at Lake Tanganyika. Here, archaeologists have found wooden clubs, spears, and other tools that show that the people lived by hunting and fishing. They also discovered evidence that fire for warmth, protection from animals, and for cooking, was used at this site.

Human skeletal remains discovered in the center of the country at Kabwe (formerly Broken Hill) show that people were living here at least 125,000 years ago.

By the late Stone Age, remains of people similar to the Bushmen, or San, were found. San still survive in small numbers throughout southern Africa. Later tools, dating about 35,000 years ago, show that the people had adapted to living in their forest environment.

The designs of some pottery made today can be traced back to Zambian civilizations from several thousand years ago.

POTTERY MAKERS

About two thousand years ago, people in this area had entered the Iron Age. They were growing food, keeping domestic animals, and forming large and complex social groups. Early Bantu migrants came into the area from the north, west, and south between the fourth and sixth centuries A.D. By the sixth century, the region northwest of Victoria Falls was settled by a migrating group from the south. All of these people, including a second wave of Bantu-speaking farmers arriving after the year 1000, have been identified by their distinctive pottery. It is possible to trace today's southern Zambian people from these groups.

Similar studies of pottery making show how the various groups of Zambia made their way into the country more than a thousand years ago. Pottery created by today's Tonga people can be traced back to that made by their ancestors in the twelfth century. Pottery styles of groups living in central and northeastern Zambia today suggest both originally lived in Shaba, the wedge of Zaire that thrusts between Zambia's east and west wings on the north. The ancestors of the various African people who live throughout Zambia today were essentially all in place more than five hundred years ago.

EXTENDED FAMILY GROUPS

In the earliest centuries, people lived in extended families and clans, groups in which all the people were related to one another. But as people began to gather in greater numbers in order to trade their natural resources for products from other cultures, they needed other ways of organizing their relationships.

AFRICAN STATES

This was the beginning of the political chieftainship system that originated in Zaire to the north, and was already in place in Zambia by the 1400s. It became the political structure that governed most people prior to the arrival of the first white people. The principal ethnic groups of Zambia can be traced back to these early kingdoms, most of them migrating out of the upper Zaire basin. From these early groups the Bemba developed in the northeast, the Tonga in the south, the Lozi in the west, and the Lunda in the northwest. Records of these systems were kept in writing by the earliest European visitors and by the oral storytelling narratives passed down from one African generation to the next. In each of these African states, detailed history was preserved by memorizing king lists, clan narratives, descendants of officeholders, and even songs and commemorative dances.

Left: Dr. David Livingstone   Right: A stamp issued in 1973, commemorating the centenary of Livingstone's death, shows him as a missionary.

TRADERS ARRIVE IN AFRICA

As remote as central Africa is today, it was even more so in the fifteenth century, yet traders from Asia and Europe had already penetrated the interior and overcome hazards to exchange their goods for the riches that Africa had to offer. The Portuguese were especially successful in traveling into central Africa and by the beginning of the eighteenth century had established trading posts along the Zambezi River. They traded for gold and exploited Zambia's elephants for their ivory. The Portuguese remained on the fringes of Zambia in the east and sought contact with different groups to promote trade.

DAVID LIVINGSTONE

The first whites living in Zambia were missionaries, and the best known of these was David Livingstone. Born in Scotland, Livingstone studied both medicine and religion in preparation for

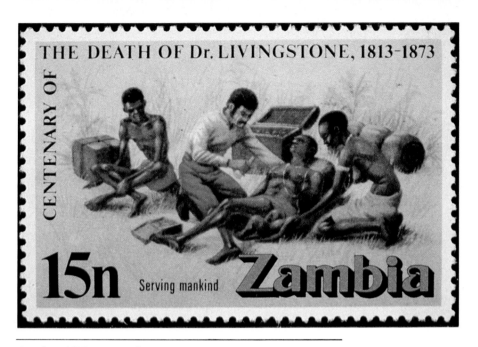

Another 1973 stamp shows Livingstone practicing medicine.

his work as a medical missionary. He immersed himself in the interior of Africa, arriving in southern Africa in 1841. He made his way to Zambia in 1851. Off and on for the next twenty-two years, until his death in 1873, Zambia was his home. Conditions in southern Africa were so perilous, Livingstone sent his wife and children home to England while he stayed on, alone, to do what he could for the local people. Their problems were many, but health and medical needs were perhaps the greatest. Livingstone shared their problems in the most personal way: his wife, Mary, died from malaria on her way to Zambia to rejoin her husband.

Living among the people and treating their illnesses, Livingstone became a keen observer of their customs. He recorded them in his book, *Missionary Travels,* and in his published journals. He observed the power that the chief held over his people and especially the cruelty practiced by the rulers over those whom they conquered. He tried to influence the way the people were treated by these conquerors, but recorded sadly in his journals that his attempts "to introduce a system of kindness" were unsuccessful.

15

Slaves were caught in the interior, yoked in pairs, and marched (left) to slave markets on the coast (right).

THE SLAVE TRADE

But soon thoughts of ivory and other exotic materials were forgotten in the rush for the most precious commodity of all: human beings. The slave trade had begun. With the expansion of sugar plantations on the island of Mauritius and in faraway Brazil, increasing numbers of African slaves were needed for labor.

Although it was the Arabs who acted as the traders, and some African chiefs themselves who permitted their people to be taken, it was the Europeans and Americans who actually bought the slaves and forced them to work for their owners' profit.

LOCAL WARS

The structure of daily life was brutally torn apart by the slave traders. But the people were subject also to local wars for power and material wealth. These local wars raged throughout the nineteenth century. More powerful groups absorbed weaker ones, increasing their numbers and their wealth. Yet all of this upheaval, pitting black against black, would soon fade before the overwhelming changes brought by the whites. The arrival of the British forever changed the lives of the people and their territory. It was the white man's thirst for land, for minerals, for a source of labor, and for power that would direct the course of Zambian history for the next century.

LIVINGSTONE EXPLORES THE ZAMBEZI RIVER

To Livingstone, slavery was a scourge, the greatest crime he encountered. It was both the worst of the problems the people suffered, and also the one he thought he could help to end. His idea seems rather innocent to us, but he believed in it completely. He was innately good and thought that he could help put an end to slavery by exposing people to modern ideas of science and commerce.

Because he was intensely interested in exploring the geography of the area, Livingstone decided to mark out trade routes and paths for those who could bring their scientific expertise to the interior. This, he thought, would open up commerce and trade for the Africans and help them resist those who paid them to sell out their own people. He made three great treks across the continent, traveling both to the west coast and to the east on different journeys. His path was the Zambezi River, which he explored for many years. He mapped nearly all of its 1,700 miles (2,736 kilometers) during his tremendously difficult journeys.

He is believed to have been the first white man to come upon

17

A nineteenth-century engraving of Victoria Falls, "the smoke that thunders"

the powerful and thrilling torrent of water that the Zambians called *mosi ao tunya*, "the smoke that thunders." The name came from the fine white spray that fills the air above the falls as the Zambezi crashes down the gorge and then continues on its long journey to the Indian Ocean. Livingstone honored the falls in his own manner, naming them for his queen, Victoria. His sketches were very precise and his measurements were remarkably accurate, detailing the dimensions of the falls. His last visit to the falls was in 1860.

Livingstone saw his explorations as the path to improving the lives of the people he had come to love. But instead of bringing in those who would uplift the people, he actually helped the slavers who used the trails he had opened. And the commerce he wanted to establish came in the form of guns, which the local chiefs were eager to obtain. Of one chief Livingstone wrote, "He had the idea that our teaching was chiefly the art of shooting . . .'' In order to get the guns, the chiefs traded some of their own people. Livingstone's writings of the life of the people in the thirty years he spent in Africa are an important source for the troubled slave trade period.

LIVINGSTONE REMEMBERED

Livingstone was unsuccessful in curtailing the slave trade and unable to overcome the people's medical problems; indeed, malaria remains a major health threat in Zambia today. But although he made little tangible improvement in the lives of the people, he made a lasting impression on their hearts and souls. Livingstone remains a beloved figure in Zambia. Schoolchildren spend a semester learning about his work in their country and his devotion to the people. He was totally committed to the people for their benefit, not his own. This made David Livingstone virtually unique among the whites who came after him. The town of Livingstone, near Victoria Falls, was named for him, and was the capital of Zambia until 1935. It is the only town with a British name that was not changed to an African name after Zambia's independence in 1964.

TROUBLE AMONG CHIEFS

Because the land was so fertile, the people were able to farm and feed themselves with little fear of food shortages. But this also made the area attractive to aggressive raiding parties. Stronger groups attacked and defeated weaker ones throughout the missionary period, before the arrival of other Europeans. The well-known English scout and hunter, Frederick Selous, encountered Chikunda parties trading and raiding for slaves among the Tonga, both of the Zambezi valley and what is now the Southern Province of Zambia. And within each grouping, there was constant agitation for loyalty to the king or chief. In 1884, the French missionary Francois Coillard came at the invitation of Lewanika to teach the people how to make better use of their land. Later, Coillard wrote, "What struck me in the king is that with many good qualities he is animated by an insatiable thirst of vengeance, and that vengeance is not wreaked on the leaders of the late revolution but on all their kin, women and children."

Such battles brought great riches to the winning chief. Lewanika, king of the Lozi, gained some twenty thousand head of cattle during one such raid. The role of the missionaries seems to have been that of court reporters; several journals and books from that time record these raids in great detail.

THE EUROPEANS ARRIVE

But there was an enemy on the horizon that would totally change the nature of politics. The question of the balance of power among the Africans soon took a distant second place to the uneven battle between black and white. The coming of the Europeans at the end of the century changed the contest entirely.

Some could see the first signs of it as early as the 1850s. In one of his books, Livingstone wrote of a warning to a chief about the coming of the Boers, the white farmers from South Africa. But in the days before any organized attempt was made by the Europeans to take over this land, the chiefs were in complete control. In the 1880s, for example, European traders had to receive

The Berlin West Africa Conference

permission from the local king to cross a river. In several journals of the time, traders and travelers wrote of waiting for weeks before permission was given. And permission was invariably accompanied by presents—of cloth, of jewelry, and of guns.

Perhaps the greatest threat to the people of Zambia came from other Africans in the distant south, the Matabele. These fierce warriors, a branch of the Zulu, were already raiding the areas close to the Lozi. But they were soon to be stopped, not by the African people whose lands they were raiding, but by the soldiers defending the white merchants who proved to be the most devastating force of all.

THE BERLIN WEST AFRICA CONFERENCE

The fate of the Lozi, and all the people of present-day Zambia, had been decided thousands of miles away, earlier in the 1880s. At the Berlin West Africa Conference of 1884-85, the European

21

powers gathered to settle the disputes over their various claims on Africa. The participants were representatives of Great Britain, France, Germany, Belgium, Portugal, Spain, Austria, Denmark, Italy, Holland, Persia, Russia, Sweden, Norway, Turkey, the United States, and the Indian Ocean island of Zanzibar. Without any discussion or consent from those they were dividing up, vast territories of Africa were "granted" to the European powers that negotiated for them. In this way, Zambia became part of the British Empire.

The actions of the Berlin Conference were clearly understood by contemporary Africans. The *Lagos Observer* (Nigeria) of February 19, 1885, wrote, "The world had, perhaps, never witnessed a robbery on so large a scale. Africa is helpless to prevent it. . . . It is on the cards that the 'Christian' business can only end, at no distant date, in the annihilation of the natives."

The conference did not actually annihilate the Africans, but it did put an end to their independence, freedom, and the space in which to develop as they chose. The "scramble for Africa" was now a matter of record.

REDRAWING BOUNDARIES

Perhaps the most lasting and most divisive legacy left by the Berlin Conference was the redrawing of Africa's boundaries. "Nations" were created for the convenience of the Europeans who were more anxious to prevent war among themselves than they were about the people whose lands they had taken. Boundaries and groupings were ignored; some lines were drawn that divided some groups, while others forced enemies into the same country. Language differences, cultural differences, religious differences—

none of these concerned the Europeans or were even noticed by them.

Although the British became the "rulers" of the territory now called Zambia, they had no actual right to the lands that made up the claim. All they had done was to eliminate the Portuguese from the scene. Now they had to deal with the chiefs who actually ruled the land and the people.

THE BRITISH SOUTH AFRICA COMPANY

Lewanika looked upon the British as protection against the Portuguese. He hoped to use this protection while he continued to receive the economic and educational benefits the missionaries had to offer. He expected to receive development aid from the British without giving up any of his power over his own people. But the document he signed, the Lochner Treaty of 1890, was not at all what he expected. Although the agreement carried the seal of Great Britain, it was actually a treaty between the Lozi king and the British South Africa Company (BSAC), a commercial enterprise. Lochner was in fact an agent of the Company, as it was known, not of the British government itself.

On October 29, 1889, Cecil Rhodes, an Englishman who had settled in present-day South Africa, had been given a royal charter for his British South Africa Company, which gave him treaty powers. He had negotiated similar treaties in southern Africa in his push to dominate commercial interests throughout the territory.

Great Britain did not have the funds to invest in these distant and difficult areas. Rhodes's wealth, earned in the diamond fields of South Africa, had tipped the scales of history in British Central

Administrators of the British South Africa Company; Cecil Rhodes is in the center.

Africa. Harry Johnston, a field man who was out securing lands for Great Britain, wrote Rhodes, "When the Government, though wishing to save this country from the Portuguese, yet had not a penny to spend on it, you stepped forward and said, 'Make the extension of British supremacy and I will find the money' and within a week . . . new instructions were drawn up for me at the Foreign Office."

Rhodes provided the money to explore and exploit this area, as well as the land to the south of the Zambezi River. He convinced his government to do so by drawing a picture of the vast new markets and new lands Africa had to offer. Without them, he said, the United Kingdom would suffer economic declines and possible lawlessness. He argued that the small islands of Great Britain were already becoming crowded with people; expanding to the vast spaces of Africa would ease the crowding and the tensions.

Rhodes's efforts to buy up concessions in Zambia turned Great Britain's "rule" over this territory from a "gentlemen's agreement" to reality.

There was no question from the start exactly what that rule would be like. It was stated in British law: "It matters not how the acquisition has been brought about. It may be by conquest, it may be by concession following a treaty . . . In all cases the result is the same . . . as regards any native inhabitant of such territories, such rights as he had under the rules of predecessors avail him nothing" and "even if in a Treaty of Cession it is stipulated that certain inhabitants should enjoy certain rights, that does not give a title to these inhabitants to enforce these stipulations." This, then, was the country that set itself off on a "civilizing" mission in Africa.

CONFLICTING TERMS OF THE LOCHNER TREATY

The Lochner Treaty provided exactly what King Lewanika had asked for—but only in the copy he received. The copy held by the BSAC eliminated key phrases. It did not state that Lewanika's authority would remain intact and it also left open the idea of the Company interfering in the internal affairs of the Lozi kingdom. Coillard and other missionaries saw the treaty as essential to protecting the missions and carrying out their plans for the area known as Barotseland. (Rotse is what the missionaries called the Lozi. They made a mistake in pronunciation and then put the mistake in writing.) They advised the king to sign and were crucial in convincing him and the other chiefs that the treaty was in their best interests.

Shortly thereafter, Lewanika repudiated the Lochner Treaty.

There were other plots afoot that showed how little concern the British had for the Lozi. Several years after signing the treaty, the king discovered that part of his kingdom had been divided between the British and the Portuguese. He pleaded with Queen Victoria in a letter: "I would like your Government to rule all my country and to save my people. I do not wish my country to be divided into two parts between Portugal and Germany."

LOZI KINGDOM COMES UNDER BRITISH RULE

In 1891, under pressure from Rhodes, the British government finally completed an agreement with Portugal and the Portuguese gave up any claim to Lozi territory. But the new boundary between western Barotseland and Portuguese Angola ran through part of Lewanika's kingdom. Back in the 1890s when the BSAC was negotiating with Lewanika for a concession that would give them rights to the minerals found in the area under his control, it was in their interest to echo Lewanika's claim for the largest area possible, so as to enhance their concession. The exact limits of Lewanika's kingdom were still in dispute well into the 1960s and still involving the same commercial company that changed the face of Zambia (and much of southern Africa): The British South Africa Company.

THE BSAC EXPANDS

Lewanika now acknowledged the Lochner Treaty and in 1898 agreed to the Lawley Concession, which gave the Company even more extensive rights. Other concessions were being granted in the eastern wing by the chiefs in power there. In 1897, the

With money provided by Cecil Rhodes, police led white settlers from South Africa to Rhodesia. There the settlers acquired the best farmland and, through the BSAC, controlled the copper mines.

territory north of the Zambezi and south of the Congo became known as Northern Rhodesia, now present-day Zambia. (The BSAC was already ruling Southern Rhodesia.)

The Bemba and the Lunda came under BSAC rule by 1899. The mineral rights to the region were secure. In 1911, an administrator for all of Northern Rhodesia set up offices at Livingstone. The Africans were forced to work for the Company, yet when the end of the Company's rule came, in 1924, virtually nothing had been done for the welfare of the people by the Company.

Unlike the territories to the south, Northern Rhodesia did not have great mineral wealth in the form of diamonds and gold. The Company was aware of the presence of copper in the northern part of the territory, although it did not know how extensive the reserves were. But the boundary between Northern Rhodesia and the Congo to the north was in dispute and that boundary ran right through the Copperbelt. Both Great Britain and Belgium claimed that section known as Katanga, the "foot" that thrusts

THE RHODES COLOSSUS
STRIDING FROM CAPE TOWN TO CAIRO.

. Mr. Rhodes had announced his intention to continue the telegraph northwards across the Zambesi to Uganda, then, crossing the Soudan, to complete the overland telegraph line from Cape Town to Cairo.

A cartoon of 1892 depicts Rhodes as one of the Seven Wonders of the Ancient World.

into Zambia today. Each had agents out in the bush trying to make deals with the chiefs who ruled the areas. Treaties were signed and then stolen. In the end, Belgium won out. Katanga became part of the Belgian Congo.

RHODES'S PLANS FOR AFRICA

That dispute was one reason why the exploitation of Northern Rhodesia's resources was delayed. But the larger reason was that Northern Rhodesia was simply a piece of a grand puzzle that Cecil Rhodes hoped to construct. Moving into Northern Rhodesia was, for Rhodes, just a stop in achieving his personal vision: to expand the presence of Great Britain ''from the Cape to Cairo.''

That was truly Rhodes's dream: to create an unbroken chain of British territory that would stretch from Cairo, Egypt, in the north of Africa all the way through the continent, down to the Cape of Good Hope, the southernmost tip. The connecting symbol would be the rail line that would permit one to travel "British" all the way.

Rhodes's success was a matter of the right man being in the right place at precisely the right time. The wealth he earned in the diamond fields of South Africa was enormous, matched only by the size of his ambitions. His money enabled him to play with the lives of millions of people. And those people meant nothing more to him than the role they might play in his plan to see Great Britain dominate all of Africa, north to south, along the eastern half of the continent.

When Rhodes acquired the land of the Lozi, Barotseland, in his first treaty north of the Zambezi, he also destroyed the Portuguese dream of extending its territory from the east coast to the west coast of southern Africa; they already had the lands that are today known as Angola and Mozambique. He came very close to achieving his dream though he did not live long enough to see how his schemes worked out. Today, English is the language spoken along that route from the Cape to Cairo.

EXPLOITATION

Although Rhodes had no need at that time for much of the land his company had acquired, this did not stand in the way of the Company's exploitation of the Africans. Since the Company had invested considerable money in purchasing some 290,000 square

The Africans lived in a cashless society (above) since they earned no wages. However, they were expected to pay a hut tax, so thousands were forced to work in mines in other countries (right).

miles (716,605 square kilometers), the land—or rather the people on it—would have to repay that investment.

The method was bureaucratic and efficient: the Company enacted a hut tax, *musonko.* The people had no way to pay this tax, since they lived in a cashless economy. They did not earn wages from doing work. They grew their own food, made their own clothing and houses, and had no need for cash. But with the hut tax, for the first time they did need money. And the only way to get it was to go to work for the white man. In this way, the whites were able to get both labor and cash from the Africans. And they were very keen to collect this tax, no matter how much hardship it caused. Thousands were forced to go to work in the mines in other countries in southern Africa.

RESISTANCE TO THE HUT TAX

The British justified the hut tax and the hardships it created by equating it with the money spent on protecting the people against slavery, rather than as what it clearly was: a fee for the right to live on the lands they had lived on for generations. But the Africans resisted this tax fiercely and the British fought back even more fiercely. People who did not pay the hut tax saw their thatch-roof houses burned to the ground by the tax collectors.

Many resisted by running away: whole villages ran away to the Belgian Congo, just to the north. For those who stayed, physical punishment was often applied. And to make sure others did not run away from forced labor—called *chibalo* by the Africans— chains were used to link men together in chain gangs.

Yet while the Africans were subject to the tax, the white settlers were not. It was not until 1921 that an income tax was applied to the whites. And even when such a tax was enacted, it was done in a manner that permitted a white to earn considerable income before he was subject to tax, whereas the hut tax was simply one month's wages. All the while the Africans were enduring the hut tax, the Company was ignoring the most valuable resource it had, quite literally under its feet—copper. Only after the end of Company rule did the exploitation of copper begin.

THE BSAC ENDS ITS RULE IN NORTHERN RHODESIA

Through the meticulous records kept by the tax collectors and by the district commissioners, the full cruelty of the British colonial system is revealed. One bureaucrat even boasted of how

31

cheaply the country could be run since, "There are no schools, no doctor . . ." It continued like this throughout the duration of the BSAC's rule, which ended in 1923.

By 1923, the BSAC was feeling pressure from the whites of Northern Rhodesia for a more direct say in governing the territory. The Company proposed joining the two Rhodesias, but the white settlers in Northern Rhodesia were opposed to this plan. They were afraid they would be dominated by those in the more advanced Southern Rhodesia. They preferred to come directly under the protection of the British government itself as a colony. And the Company had grown tired of its self-imposed burdens in Northern Rhodesia. So it was that in 1924, the rule of the British South Africa Company came to an end after twenty-nine years.

But the legacy Rhodes and the BSAC left behind continued. At the beginning of his push into the territory he wrote, "Either you have to receive them on an equal footing as citizens or you have to call them a subject race. Well, I have made up my mind that there must be class legislation, that there must be Pass Laws and Peace Preservation Acts, and that we have got to treat natives when they are in a state of barbarism, in a different way from ourselves." How would Rhodes have explained the trip that Lewanika made to England in 1901 to attend the coronation of Edward VII? Lewanika truly believed he was dealing with the British as an equal.

The Company's final gesture was to give up to Britain's colonial office all rights to the territory—except mineral rights. The best chance Northern Rhodesia had for achieving financial security was left in the hands of the BSAC, and it would profit enormously from this in the decades to come.

Chapter 3
STRUGGLES FOR
INDEPENDENCE

A BRITISH COLONY

For the Africans, the change from Company rule to direct British rule on April 1, 1924 proved to be a step backward. Sir Herbert Stanley, the first governor appointed by the colonial office to govern Northern Rhodesia, saw his territory as a "white man's country" that would help unite Southern Rhodesia and South Africa with British East Africa.

In a misguided attempt to encourage white immigration, sixty thousand Africans were forced to move off their lands to accommodate white settlers. This was the beginning of the decline of African agriculture in the territory. The expected surge of settlers did not materialize, however. Life in Northern Rhodesia was too much of a risk. Malaria and sleeping sickness were two of the often fatal diseases that were prevalent.

THE COPPER INDUSTRY

When the whites did come, it was to the copper mines, which began operating on a large scale in the mid-1920s. By the early

An open pit copper mine

1930s copper had assumed a dominant role in Northern Rhodesia, the same role, in fact, that it continues to play today. The lack of planning for the territory by both the BSAC and the British government is clear from Zambia's continued dependence on copper. Unfortunately, even twenty-five years of independence have not changed this economic fact.

The railroads that were built to serve the mining industries in other countries in southern Africa were now at the service of the fledgling copper industry. They acted as a magnet for people, both black and white, and saw the beginning of a highly urbanized population, the most urbanized in black Africa. Half the white settlers, who numbered more than fourteen thousand in 1931, were concentrated in the Copperbelt. The Africans followed them, desperate for work that would enable them to pay the hut tax and to buy food they no longer grew. Even when there was not any paid work available, people were still being put in prison because they did not pay the tax. By 1936, when the copper mines had been producing for more than ten years, the hut tax still accounted for 13 percent of the colony's total revenue.

PROSPERITY ONLY FOR THE WHITES

While the whites prospered under the economic bonanza that copper brought, the colonial office continued to ignore the basic needs of the Africans. Schooling was left to the missions, which were far too few to handle the job. When Northern Rhodesia gained independence, it was left with the poorest educational system of any British colony in modern times. This lack of schooling guaranteed that blacks could not compete for any of the better jobs that were available in the Copperbelt. Neither they nor their interests were represented in the colony's legislature.

CHIEFS TAKE PART IN THE COLONIAL ADMINISTRATION

In 1932 an effort was made to bring the Africans into the decision-making process. The idea was to have chiefs from each area become part of the colonial administration, leading eventually to self-rule. Governor J.M. Maxwell began the effort and by 1936 it was in practice throughout the territory. The results were dismaying. The people distrusted the chiefs who became part of the same system that had caused them so much grief. Among groups such as the Tonga who had never had chiefs, the colonial officials created chieftainships and then chose chiefs to fill the positions. It is not surprising that these made-up chiefs had no real standing among the people and were neither trusted nor respected.

Meanwhile, the whites were having their own problems. Although the British government in reality did little for the Africans, its official view was that the Africans' interests were the first priority, over the settlers'. The settlers reacted by strengthening their ties with the whites of Southern Rhodesia. Although no union would take place yet, the seeds were sown.

NEW INSTITUTIONS GAIN INFLUENCE

With the chiefs now drafted into the government, the people were left to drift. Many institutions moved in to fill the need for trusted authority figures. Among the religious movements that took advantage of this situation was the Jehovah's Witnesses, a religious sect that rejected alien political authority. They preached nonpayment of taxes and nonrecognition of authority.

Other Christian groups also became more important during this era. Self-help groups were formed to provide for the people's needs, especially in the rural areas. Many unions also were formed during this period, although they did not succeed in gaining much power. Later in the country's history, however, they would play an important role. Nationalist political parties sprouted during this period as well. And with each new level of grassroots organization, the government would attempt to bring the groups into the official structure.

In 1938 the government introduced urban courts and urban advisory councils involving counselors and elders representing the various people. Regional provincial councils were established in 1944. But all of these were designed to keep the Africans from living their own lives, free of outside control, and failed to give back to the people what had been taken from them.

WHITES FEAR AFRICAN MAJORITY RULE

The whites, who had earlier feared union with Southern Rhodesia, now saw this alliance as the only alternative to African majority rule that they feared even more. Their counterparts in Southern Rhodesia were now more eager for union with the north for different reasons. They were afraid that the Afrikaners, the Dutch-speaking whites who had gained power in South Africa in 1948, would also take over in Southern Rhodesia. In time, they believed they would lose their connection with the English-speaking world.

The Africans greatly feared any kind of union, for they saw it would give the whites even more power. The inclusion of a third territory, Nyasaland, as part of a new Federation, was more than a matter of tidy bookkeeping for the Europeans; it was a source of cheap migrant labor.

CENTRAL AFRICAN FEDERATION IS FORMED

Although the British government had resisted the pleas of the whites for a union, the change in power in Great Britain in 1951 changed the mood. Over the protests of several African organizations, including the Northern Rhodesian African National Congress, the African Representative Council, and many of the self-help associations, discussions and conferences went ahead. The whites carried the day; on August 1, 1953, the Central African Federation was formed. The British government backed Federation largely for economic reasons and ignored African objections. It consisted of the two Rhodesias and Nyasaland. Barotseland, the home of the Lozi, was set aside as a special area within the Federation. Godfrey Huggins was named federal prime minister. He was succeeded in 1956 by Roy Welensky.

Although the Federation was described as a partnership between whites and blacks, only six of the thirty-six members of the new Parliament were black. Salisbury, the capital of Southern Rhodesia, was designated as the capital of the Federation, an indication that the partnership also was unequal between the two Rhodesias. The differences between Northern and Southern Rhodesia would grow greater during the period of Federation, which was just another form of British control over the territories.

DOMINANCE OF SOUTHERN RHODESIA

Partnership was the slogan of the Central African Federation, a partnership between blacks and whites. For both the blacks and the whites of Northern Rhodesia, however, the scales were tilted very much in favor of Southern Rhodesia. The whites in both Rhodesias viewed Federation as a way of denying the blacks any significant say in governing themselves. It also provided a way for the whites of Southern Rhodesia to profit from the income generated by the Copperbelt.

The Africans fought against Federation, fearing it would make it even more difficult for them to ever achieve independence and majority rule. The Federation's legislature showed just what sort of a "partnership" the whites had in mind: only six of its thirty-six members could be African, by law. Most of the white members in the legislature were from Southern Rhodesia.

Soon after Federation, it was decided to place the Federation capital at Salisbury, already the capital of Southern Rhodesia. All the benefits of having a capital city went to Southern Rhodesia at the expense of Northern Rhodesia. Salisbury (now Harare) grew enormously as corporate and government offices established their headquarters there. The facilities built in Northern Rhodesia simply decayed from disuse. The blacks called Salisbury *bamba zonke*, "take all." It was an apt nickname.

CREATION OF LAKE KARIBA

The bias toward Southern Rhodesia was clear, but it was about to become a great deal clearer. At the time of Federation, the member states had signed an agreement to build a dam that would generate electricity for the whole community. The dam was to be built on the Kafue River in Northern Rhodesia, which had the potential for irrigation. Work actually started on the Kafue project. But those in Southern Rhodesia wanted more control over the project. They also were looking for a project that would bring prestige to the Federation.

By creating the largest man-made lake in the world at Kariba on the Zambezi River, they expected to do just that. The enormous amount of money needed to build at Kariba came largely from Northern Rhodesia's Copperbelt earnings and, not surprisingly, the mining groups refused to participate. But the Federation's prime minister, Lord Malvern, gave them no choice. If they did not support the project, a huge export tax would be placed on every ton of copper shipped out of the country. They gave in. The dam was built on the Zambezi.

The power plant was on the southern bank of the river, in Southern Rhodesia. One "partner" was going behind the other's back to secure benefits for itself. The dam made the Federation self-sufficient in electricity, a tremendous advantage for any

When Lake Kariba was formed, a game rescue operation went to work, saving stranded animals from the rising waters. In the photograph above, game department workers secure a zebra to their boat for transfer to a new, safe location.

country. But it also proved that Southern Rhodesia would do anything to prosper at the expense of the north. White support for Federation was dealt a major blow. It was clear that joining with Southern Rhodesia to maintain white control had many hidden costs for Northern Rhodesia.

INEQUITIES OF THE FEDERATION

Roy Welensky took charge of the Federation in 1956. He worked to gain even more power for the white-ruled legislature and greater independence from the British colonial office, which still controlled Northern Rhodesia. He had two goals: to prevent the breakup of the Federation and to prevent black majority control. But the absurdly uneven treatment of Northern Rhodesia by the Federation made such a breakup inevitable. The two major partners in the Federation were drawing farther apart. In

Southern Rhodesia, the white liberal government head, Garfield Todd, lost power. Southern Rhodesia became even more opposed to black majority rule under its new prime minister, Ian Smith.

Life for the blacks in Northern Rhodesia was a series of discriminations. They could not go to the theater or cinema. They could not enter or use hotels or cafés. It took a series of peaceful protests before they gained the right to enter cafés and cinemas in 1960. But they remained far behind whites in the salaries they earned, even when they were able to take over jobs formerly reserved for whites. In 1953, the average European salary was fifteen times that of the average African. By 1960 the average African salary had more than doubled, but it was still barely a tenth that of the average European.

The whites said blacks did not have the education to get better jobs or better wages, but then made sure they did not have the schools to get the education they needed. In 1958, only one thousand Africans were enrolled in secondary schools that offered the equivalent of only a second-year high school education. There was no university at all in Northern Rhodesia.

BLACKS BEGIN TO ORGANIZE

While the whites fretted under Federation, the blacks began to organize. The Northern Rhodesian Congress, a black group that had fought against Federation, was renamed the African National Congress (ANC) in 1951. It was a regional group and Kenneth Kaunda was a member.

But in 1958, Kaunda and others split from the ANC and formed a new party called the Zambia African National Congress (ZANC). It was the first time the name Zambia, derived from the

Zambezi River, was used. Kaunda was named president of this group. The group was banned by the governor of Northern Rhodesia in 1959, and its leaders, including Kaunda were arrested and sent to distant parts of the country to prevent them from influencing the Africans. But the blacks struggling for independence created another group in its place: the United National Independence Party (UNIP), and when Kaunda was released from jail, he was elected as its president.

ELECTIONS ARE HELD IN NORTHERN RHODESIA

By 1960, the doubtful future of the Federation had become evident even to the British government. The whites in Northern Rhodesia were agitating for self-government under white rule, but that was asking the British government to create independence for a country in which power was in the hands of a tiny minority. Instead, elections were held.

In October 1962, Africans and Europeans met face to face at a nationwide Northern Rhodesia election. Kaunda's party united with the opposition black group and achieved an African majority.

FEDERATION ENDS

The end of Federation was the next step. On December 31, 1963, it was dissolved by the British government. In January of 1964, Kaunda became prime minister of the first cabinet dominated by Africans. Even the paramount chief of the Lozi threw his support to UNIP and finally, though reluctantly, agreed to allow Barotseland to become a fully integrated part of the new country to be known as Zambia.

Left: Dr. Kenneth D. Kaunda, with his wife, became the first president of Zambia.
Right: A traditional dance performed during independence celebrations

INDEPENDENCE FOR ZAMBIA

A series of issues were negotiated during 1964, leading up to independence on October 24, 1964. Kenneth Kaunda, who had played a major role in helping to achieve independence for Zambia, was elected president of the new nation.

Only eleven years had passed since the whites had pushed through Federation. They had held off black majority rule in Northern Rhodesia, but at a great cost to their own best interests. Nyasaland, the often forgotten third member of the Federation, was declared the independent state of Malawi on July 6, 1964.

BSAC LOSES MINERAL RIGHTS

One important matter remained unresolved. The British South

Africa Company, once the governing body in the territory, had retained mineral rights through all the years of Northern Rhodesia's status as a Crown Colony and during Federation. BSAC earned enormous royalties from the mines each year. During months of negotiations, a major study of the original agreements that led to BSAC ownership of those rights led to the conclusion that their claims were based on very faulty documents. Just before independence, BSAC agreed to give up all mineral rights for one payment of just $12 million. All the money earned from copper would now go into Zambia's treasury. The new government would start life on a strong financial basis.

IAN SMITH DECLARES SOUTHERN RHODESIA'S INDEPENDENCE

With Federation now dissolved, Southern Rhodesia was the only part of the territory still totally committed to white minority rule. Resisting the British government's plans that would lead the country to black majority rule, Prime Minister Ian Smith took an unprecedented step. On November 11, 1965, he simply declared that Southern Rhodesia was independent. The move was completely illegal, but Smith was a strong and determined leader and violently opposed to the blacks. How could the north move peacefully to black majority rule, while the south dug its heels in and refused to follow Britain's decision?

Smith had a very committed following of whites, a quarter million of them. In England itself, many might have been on the lowest level of poor white society. In Africa, they were the ruling elite. They were willing to fight to preserve their way of life. And that decision would prove very costly for Zambia.

Chapter 4

AN INDEPENDENT NATION

KENNETH KAUNDA, STATESMAN

How does a man become the first president of a country? There is no blueprint. For Kenneth Kaunda, as for most African leaders, the path was full of obstacles. A happy ending was certainly not assured. Kaunda was just forty years old when Zambia became independent. He had some experience in the running of a political organization, but certainly not in governing a nation of more than 3.5 million people. He inherited a country in which a tiny minority enjoyed a privileged life, while the vast majority was considered inferior. He had to run a country that, at independence, had very few educated people.

He turned out to be precisely the right man for the job. In a nation with more than seventy ethnic groups, he had no strong ethnic identity. This kept him from becoming identified with one group in preference to another. Although he was born in the little town of Lubwa in the northern part of what was then Northern Rhodesia, Kaunda's parents were from Malawi. He had little time to be a child, for his father, an African missionary, died when Kaunda was eight. Immediately, he began working in order to pay for his own school fees. His education was in the hands of the missionaries, who were a great influence in his life. He struggled to stay in school for as long as he could, but even before finishing secondary school he was called back to Lubwa to begin teaching others.

For the next eight years he taught, first at Lubwa, then in Tanganyika and Southern Rhodesia. It was in Southern Rhodesia that he first encountered blatant racial discrimination. As a black he had to carry a pass that proved he had a right to be in certain areas. He very soon returned to Northern Rhodesia where he became boarding master at a school on the Copperbelt, at Mufulira. His wife, Betty, taught the younger grades at the same school. His teaching was always aimed at helping people to become independent. At school, he helped the students grow vegetables so they could earn money to pay their school fees.

While teaching, Kaunda became involved with the local self-help association, which was the beginning of his political activity. It was here that he was elected to the provincial council. This was the only place he could begin to work against the discrimination suffered by Africans in their own country.

When he decided to return to farming, which he loved, in 1949, he became even more active in these local organizations. It was difficult for Kaunda to take care of his growing family. He farmed; he sold secondhand clothes; and he did some teaching as well. He was always a humble man, one who never let pride get in the way of what had to be done. But it was clear that organized activity would be necessary if the Africans ever were going to take their rightful place in Northern Rhodesia. Kaunda had studied the methods of Gandhi and Nehru in India. He knew that the British colonies in Asia were gaining their independence. Yet at the same

President Kenneth Kaunda

time, the whites in Northern Rhodesia were fighting that trend and urging the British government to allow them to create the Central African Federation. Kaunda and his friends knew that such a federation would make it even more difficult for them to ever achieve independence and majority rule. They organized a local branch of the ANC and traveled around the Northern Province by bicycle to promote it among the farming community. Women had an important role in the nationalist parties, although this went against traditional African practices. But the party leaders realized that if they eliminated women, half the adult population would have no part to play in the fight for independence.

The main goal of the ANC was to protest against the union of Northern Rhodesia, Southern Rhodesia, and Nyasaland into Federation. They did not succeed, and when Federation was declared on August 1, 1953, the previous leaders of the ANC were overthrown. Kaunda was elected secretary-general and moved from his farm to Lusaka. He was farther along the path to becoming leader of Zambia than anyone could have realized at the time.

Shortly after Federation was announced, Kaunda wrote, "In central Africa a major constitutional change has been imposed against the expressed wish of some six million Africans in favor of a handful of reactionary white settlers. This imposition has only been possible because the imperialists count on the strength of the British troops, which they are ruthlessly using in crushing down the national aspirations of the colonial peoples . . . they have only managed to shelve the inevitable racial strike in central Africa. Serious trouble lies ahead. The imposition of Federation has made this trouble more certain than ever."

A brief imprisonment in 1955 for possessing prohibited literature gave Kaunda the "stamp of approval" that was earned by most leaders in the moves toward independence. It was almost impossible for any black who opposed the colonial system to avoid prison. The literature that was considered so dangerous concerned the passive resistance campaigns used by Gandhi and Nehru to achieve independence for India.

In 1957, Kaunda traveled out of Africa for the first time. He went to Britain to protest granting the Federation dominion status, a move the whites wanted to strengthen their hold on power. Through his eight-month stay in England, and throughout the decade of Federation, Kaunda broadened his understanding of the world and of other nations in Africa that had already achieved independence. All of this became part of his plans for the future of Northern Rhodesia. He hoped to take advantage of what he learned and to avoid making the same mistakes others made when they were finally granted control of their own destiny.

With opposition to Federation growing, the white government took strong steps to remain in control. In 1959, Southern Rhodesia declared a state of emergency. In Northern Rhodesia, the Zambia ANC was banned and all political leaders including Kaunda were arrested. They were sent to remote districts, each far from home, a form of self-imprisonment. This was soon changed to a sentence at Lusaka Central Prison and eventually to Salisbury Prison in Southern Rhodesia, the Federation capital. Kaunda was released in January 1960. During his imprisonment, a new party had emerged in Zambia, the United National Independence Party (UNIP).

The efforts of Kaunda and UNIP now began to be assisted by Great Britain, which finally realized that the national liberation movements taking place all over Africa could no longer be denied. The whites, desperately trying to keep their hold on the governments of Southern and Northern Rhodesia, were fighting a losing battle. An example was very close at hand.

The huge nation of the Belgian Congo, which formed a long border to the north with Northern Rhodesia, became independent on June 30, 1960. (Its name was changed to Zaire a few years later.) But the battle for independence was especially complicated because of the Federation. The whites in Southern Rhodesia were much stronger in their resistance. Northern Rhodesia had to fight its way free of both Federation and the whites in order to achieve independence.

During the several years leading up to independence, Kaunda preached a philosophy of nonviolence while still advocating an overthrow of the government. This was to be accomplished by attacking property, not the white settlers. Finally, plans for independence went ahead. A national government had to be

The British flag is taken down for the last time.

created where none had existed among the blacks before. On October 24, 1964, the new Zambian flag was raised: a green background representing the land with an orange-colored eagle, and three stripes of red, black, and orange. The black represents the people; the red is for the struggle for independence; the orange represents the nation's mineral wealth, copper; and the eagle represents the soaring hopes of the people.

A WEAK ECONOMY

At independence, President Kaunda and his fellow Zambians took control of a very weak economy. Though they had been spared the ravages of war that destroyed many of the facilities in Southern Rhodesia during its struggle to achieve independence as

Peasant farmers barely raise enough to feed themselves, but they try to sell some produce at roadside stands to get badly needed cash.

Zimbabwe, they were faced with the reality of a nation whose earnings were dependent almost entirely on copper. The economy needed desperately to be diversified. Kaunda had seen the effects of high unemployment on the Copperbelt.

Yet the agricultural sector had been neglected in favor of the mines. Many Africans had been pushed off their land. Thousands of others had flocked to the mines and the towns around them. Sixty percent of the population was involved with agriculture, but for most of the blacks, this meant subsistence farming. These peasant farmers grew food for their own needs.

Most of the big commercial farms were operated by people from outside the country. They grew virtually all the food that was sold for profit. Their farms fed those employed in the mining industry and the city dwellers.

AN ENEMY ON ZAMBIA'S BORDER

There was so much to do, so many changes to make, and such enthusiasm for the future. Copper earnings were still high enough

Ian Smith (center) attends a ceremony in 1978.

to support Kaunda's plans to make a better life for the Zambians. The success of the agricultural sector made it clear that food would not be a problem. These were enormous advantages for a new African nation. But with the declaration by Ian Smith in 1965 that Southern Rhodesia would remain a white-ruled country, Zambia was now faced with an enemy at its border—an enemy that controlled the transport of its goods and therefore, much of its economy.

SANCTIONS AGAINST RHODESIA

Great Britain, which had ultimate responsibility for Southern Rhodesia, did not send in troops to force the Europeans to surrender power. Instead, economic sanctions were declared. The British had been unwilling to face reality in Rhodesia throughout its history. They had been wrong about this region many times before; now, they thought the sanctions "would bring the nation to its knees in a matter of weeks."

Instead, the whites of Southern Rhodesia looked upon sanctions as a challenge and set about to create industries that would

Hydroelectric plant at Kariba Dam

produce nearly everything they could no longer buy from outside. Gasoline was the one crucial item they could not produce and that was supplied by South Africa, which was happy to help the whites stay in power. Any black resistance to the whites had been broken and black leaders had been jailed to prevent them from opposing the whites. It took many years before they could put up a vigorous fight against the whites.

In the meantime, Zambia had to deal with this new situation. And it was Zambia that suffered from the sanctions imposed on Rhodesia. It was through Rhodesia that Zambia's copper was shipped. The two economies had many ties resulting from the Federation period. The whole electrical network for Zambia came from the power plant located on the southern shore of Lake Kariba in Rhodesian territory. Ninety-five percent of Zambia's trade involved transportation ties with Rhodesia. Immediately, Zambia had to spend more money on transportation, money that was needed to build up the country. It cost much more to ship goods by longer and more difficult routes. In instances where there were no alternate routes, shortages occurred. Just to get fuel into the country was a major drain on the economy.

Zambia is improving its roads.

BUILDING A PIPELINE AND A RAILWAY

In order to make Zambia completely independent of Rhodesia, two important projects were begun right away. An oil pipeline was needed to bring fuel in from Dar es Salaam in Tanzania, the nearest port that was on friendly terms with Zambia. That was more than 1,000 miles (1,609 kilometers) away. It took three years for the pipeline to be built. An Italian company built it and provided financing, with interest, for the cost of construction. But during those three years, oil had to be brought in by truck along the Great North Road, also from Dar es Salaam. This road was great in name only. The truck drivers whose vehicles survived the trek called it "Hell Run." The road was not paved. It was a dirt road that became a mud road during the rainy seasons. Plenty of trucks did not make it and their abandoned wrecks could be seen all along the way.

A freight train on the outskirts of Lusaka

While the pipeline took care of the oil transportation problem, a much better and more permanent route than the road had to be created to transport goods. For this a rail line was needed. Although Zambia had an extensive railroad system, all the lines were for internal transport or were linked up with unfriendly neighboring countries. What was needed was a line that followed the oil pipeline, all the way to Dar es Salaam. Zambia's partner in this project was the People's Republic of China, the only nation that offered to build the railway and to provide a huge loan, without interest, that could be paid back over a long period. Kaunda had looked to many countries for help with the railroad, but no other country was willing to undertake the project. Although he was concerned about being in China's debt, Kaunda finally accepted the offer. Thousands of jobs were created for Africans during the construction of the railway. More than eight thousand Chinese came to Zambia to work on that section of the line. The railroad, which was built ahead of schedule, has several names: officially it is the Great Uhuru Railway (*uhuru* means "freedom" in Swahili, the language of Tanzania). It is also called the Tan-Zam or Tazara railway.

NEED FOR ELECTRICAL POWER

Ian Smith's "independence" left Zambia in a precarious position as far as electrical power was concerned. All of its electricity came from Kariba. Once again Zambia was reminded of the way Rhodesia had benefited from Federation at Zambia's expense. If the dam had been built on the Kafue River in Zambia as had been planned originally, it would not now be totally dependent on Rhodesia for its power.

Work resumed on the abandoned Kafue project. By 1972, the plant was fully operational. But for the seven years that it took before this work was completed, Zambia's sole source of electrical power could have been cut off. While most of the people in Zambia did not have electricity in their homes—most still don't—without electricity the copper industry would have been shut down entirely.

All the money that had to be put into these projects, and many others, meant that many of Zambia's other needs were virtually ignored. Building up the school system was one of the president's chief priorities, but there just wasn't enough money to do it quickly. Health clinics and clean water sources were needed. Trained people were scarce in every profession. And, there was another threat to both the country's social progress as well as to its internal security.

REFUGEES FLEE TO ZAMBIA

While Zambia had been spared a civil war on its road to independence, the situation in Rhodesia brought more than economic hardship. Shortly after Smith's declaration, Zambia became a refuge for the Rhodesian blacks whose own nationalist movements were banned. Kaunda had pledged to help his fellow Africans in their struggles against minority rule, but the price was high. The presence of these groups in Zambia brought attacks across the border. But Kaunda was committed, as was clear from the Lusaka Manifesto, a statement issued jointly by him and President Julius Nyerere of Tanzania in 1966.

> "If peaceful progress to emancipation were possible, or if changed circumstances were to make it possible in the future, we would urge our brothers in the resistance movements to use peaceful methods of struggle even at the cost of some compromise on the timing of change. But while peaceful progress is blocked by actions of those at present in power in the States of Southern Africa, we have no choice but to give to the peoples of those territories all the support of which we are capable in their struggle against their oppressors."

These were the only alternatives; remaining under white rule was *not* an alternative.

Liberation wars also were being fought on Zambia's east and west borders. In both Mozambique and Angola, wars were being carried out against their colonial ruler, Portugal. Zambia became a shelter for the freedom fighters from those two countries and, as a result, suffered attacks on her own land.

There was little of Zambia's border that was secure. And all of these wars meant that people were being driven out of their villages. Thousands of people fled, and many of them, especially those who lived close to the border, spilled into Zambia. Kaunda welcomed them and insisted that his country would give them shelter. This also cost the people and the country dearly. Kaunda had to pour money into an army to protect his borders against the soldiers of Rhodesia who would cross over in pursuit of the resistance fighters.

KAUNDA'S "HUMANISM"

While he was dealing with these disruptive forces outside Zambia's borders, President Kaunda was trying also to set the country on a new moral path, a philosophy of African Socialism he called "Humanism." He hoped to see progress in his country without a rush toward material things, yet just the opposite was happening. The cities were becoming more crowded and there were more people unemployed. He wanted to change the distribution of wealth that was so one-sided when he took office. But in fact the changes that did take place were just as lopsided. Miners were earning much more money but the peasant farmers, who made up most of the population, were scarcely earning any more than they had before. And when price raises were taken into consideration, they weren't any better off than at independence.

The situation was made even worse by the appearance of a black elite who were making as much profit as they could for their own personal enjoyment. Kaunda, a man of simple tastes, disapproved of this need for more and more possessions and wealth.

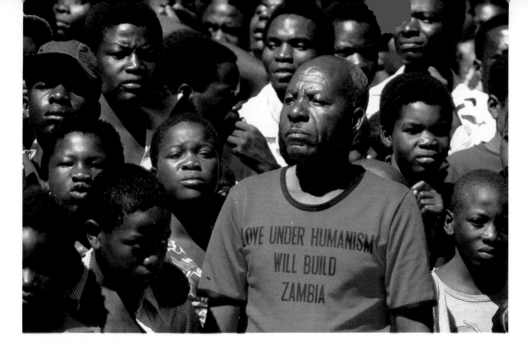

On April 19, 1968, Kaunda began to nationalize certain foreign-owned companies, both in commerce and in industry. On August 11, 1969, he went much further. The government took a 51 percent controlling interest in the copper companies. Yet with all this new control, the problems that Zambia inherited from the colonial administration were proving very difficult to solve. And all of this was made even more difficult by Zambia's very high birthrate. It was not possible to improve living conditions when so many more facilities were needed every year.

COPPER MARKET COLLAPSES

By the early 1970s, the price of copper, the backbone of Zambia's economy, collapsed. All the plans for the country had assumed that the money earned from copper exports would stay as high as it had been. As the country moved into the 1970s, it had many new problems and far less money to deal with them than it had at independence. The future did not look bright. It was ironic that the name given to Zambia's money, the *kwacha*, means "dawn" or "freedom."

The mining of copper is done both above ground in mechanized strip mines (above), and by human labor in underground mines (below).

Chapter 5

COMMERCE AND
INDUSTRY

COPPER

Copper has played the single most important role in shaping
the people and the life of Zambia. As soon as copper mining
began in the 1920s, people began traveling to the Copperbelt to
work. The railroads were built to serve the copper industry. Cities
grew up along the rail lines. The Zambian people began to live
two very different kinds of lives, the urbanized mine worker's life
or the African farmer's life. And Zambia's economy came to
depend almost entirely on the earnings from copper. Copper was
the one element on which everyone could depend.

Even in the mid-1980s, copper still accounted for 95 percent of
Zambia's foreign exchange. But now, the world market price for
copper has fallen dramatically. Copper isn't in demand as much as
it was in the past. Changing technologies have eliminated the use
of copper in certain industries. For a country that depended so
much on copper, this has been a devastating blow. All of the
country's efforts to improve the lives of its people have been
affected by the falling price of copper.

But even if the price had not fallen, copper could not support
Zambia forever. The country's copper reserves will be worked out
in about twenty years. What will remain in the ground after that

is very low-grade copper. That means there is less copper in each ton of ore that is brought to the surface. It takes more work to get the same amount of copper, so the mining process becomes more expensive. Sometimes it costs more to mine the copper than it can be sold for on world metal markets. Because of a temporary world shortage of copper, at the beginning of 1989 copper was selling for more than $1.70 a pound, three times the price it brought in the early 1980s. But even this increase was small compared to the price for gold, which was selling for around $400 an *ounce*. The labor costs are not much different, for it takes the same kind of effort to mine both. Everyone knows that Zambia must build up other areas of its economy, especially agriculture, to take the place of the money it gets from copper. But for now, copper remains king in Zambia.

Copper has always been known to the people of Zambia. Copper bracelets were found at archaeological sites, indicating that copper was worked and treasured by the people in the area as many as two thousand years ago. Traditional mining and smelting methods were used long before the white settlers began to mine copper in the 1920s. The area in which copper is found runs along Zambia's northern border, where the northern wing of the butterfly begins. This is the Copperbelt Province, and the Copperbelt itself.

Copper is found in an area that measures about 90 miles (145 kilometers) long by 30 miles (48 kilometers) wide. It is here that most of the mines were established in the 1920s and 1930s. There are two kinds of mining operations here: open pit and underground. The open pit mines, also called strip mines, are so big that trucks can be driven down into them along sloping roads to the area where the copper-bearing ore is found. To get to work

Blasting at an open pit mine

in the underground mines, the workers enter huge metal cages
that operate much like ordinary passenger elevators, except that
water is always dropping into them and the shaft is dark as they
drop deep into the earth. Once the miners reach the working level,
they walk along the tunnels until they reach the mining area. The
very old mines are more expensive to operate because the miners
must go deeper and deeper to bring up the ore and because the
ore is of a lower grade. In both operations, the miners drill holes
into the ore, place sticks of dynamite in the holes, and then leave
the mining site. When the area is clear, the blast is set off and the
ore is blasted free. The miners return to the site and load up the
ore, which is then taken to a processing plant.

In 1924, shortly after the area began to be worked, there were
1,300 Africans working on the Copperbelt; by 1930, the number
had expanded to 30,000. Then in 1931, with the worldwide
depression, there was a tremendous slump in demand, and the

Cobalt, a valuable by-product of copper processing

number of workers fell back to 13,800. With increased demand in World War II, the number of workers increased dramatically.

In 1970, the Zambian government began to take control of the mines that had been owned and operated by private companies. At this time, the industry was producing more than 700,000 tons (over 635 million kilograms) of copper a year. Shortly thereafter, another shift in demand occurred, and the number of workers dropped again. At the same time Zambia suffered from the worldwide increase in oil prices, which ate up much of its earnings. By the mid-1980s, production was down to 500,000 tons (over 450 million kilograms) a year. Today there are about 57,000 mine workers, most of them in the copper mines.

The mining of copper is only the first phase of the process. After the ore is blasted free and transported on big trucks, it is brought to the processing plant. Here, the ore is crushed and put through a concentrator. This releases the particles of copper from the waste material and from the other minerals that are found with the copper such as nickel, iron, and cobalt. (Cobalt is a very valuable by-product of copper processing.) Then the copper ore reaches the smelter where the copper is purified. This copper, now at least 99 percent pure, also may be put through an electrolytic refining process to make it even purer. Finally, it is poured into molds and allowed to cool and harden before it is shipped.

Although copper is very important to Zambia, Zambia is not as important to the world of copper. It ranks fifth in the world in production, supplying about 5 percent of all the copper sold. Chile is first in copper production, followed by the United States, the U.S.S.R., and Canada. Zaire, Zambia's northern neighbor, ranks sixth. Zambia also mines tin and small amounts of silver, selenium, and gold.

EMERALDS

The one commodity that Zambia could profit from is emeralds, the beautiful green stones that are so highly valued. While copper costs about $1.70 a pound, an emerald that could be set into a ring and weighs just a fraction of an ounce, can cost hundreds or even thousands of dollars. Zambian emeralds are well known in the world of gems, and are prized for their deep forest-green color. Although there are many emeralds mined in Zambia, virtually all of the mining is done illegally and the stones are smuggled out of the country. At one time people from Senegal were so heavily involved in this illicit trade they used their profits to build fine houses for themselves around Kitwe, in the Copperbelt. The emeralds occur naturally along with the copper. The government's office in charge of mining had not been able to control the mining and has not been able to profit from it even when the stones come into its hands.

LONRHO

One company that has flourished in Zambia for about seventy years is Lonrho, Africa's largest food producing company. The company was founded by Cecil Rhodes. Well experienced in dealing with African styles of management and shifts in government, Lonrho has been able to weather the restrictions on private companies and today has a hand in much of the country's agriculture and industry.

Its business in Zambia includes Kalangwa Estates, a cattle estate; a cotton ginnery in Mumbwa; Power Equipment, which supplies equipment for agriculture; Delkins Construction Co.; Turnpan Zambia, which supplies machinery to the mining industry; a paint manufacturer; a brewery; management of the Lusaka Hotel; Lonrho Zambia, which distributes automobiles including Toyota, Fiat, and Land Rovers, as well as spare parts; a new joint venture with the government of Zambia to promote the mining and marketing of amethysts; and the *Coca-Cola* bottler.

But the *Coca-Cola* plant demonstrates Zambia's constant problem with its economy. Whenever companies or people want to buy something that is made outside Zambia, they have to get foreign currency. Zambian currency is not valued outside the country. And Zambia does not earn enough foreign currency to buy everything people want. When a product is not considered important to the economy, it becomes more difficult to get the foreign currency. That is what happened with *Coca-Cola*. Katherine Mupotola, a young woman from Ndola says, ''There isn't any more *Coca-Cola* bottled here now because we can't get the concentrate that it's made from.'' Instead, the bottling plant is now making fruit-flavored soft drinks called Tip Top and Quench.

Cotton grown in the Gwembe area (left) is used at Kafue Textiles to make cotton cloth.

UNEMPLOYMENT

Each year, Zambia's young people flood into the urban areas looking for work, but there is not nearly enough employment for more than a small fraction of them. Moreover, since the country has not been able to move ahead as rapidly as it would like in its education program, most young Zambians leave school with less than a high school education. The only jobs they are suited for are those that require little education, such as in mining—but mining is an industry without a future and one that does not need as many people as it once did.

OTHER INDUSTRIES

There are a number of small manufacturing facilities in Zambia and a few large ones as well. With the cotton that is grown locally, local textile mills such as Kafue Textiles produce cotton cloth for

Some industries in Zambia include the Livingstone Car Plant (left), Sanpoo Industries (center), and Bata Shoes (right).

domestic use. Bata Shoes, the best-known shoe company in black Africa, has a big shoe factory in Zambia. It uses hides from Zambia's cattle to produce casual, inexpensive shoes. Another plant in the industrial area on the outskirts of Lusaka, Sanpoo Industries, makes decorative objects and classroom chalk from plaster of paris. There is a jewelry firm, Zuva Ltd., making silver jewelry set with beautiful colored gemstones. The silver and the stones are all locally mined. Each plant employs a small number of people who are taught the techniques to run the machinery and make the finished product.

There are also large-scale operations that make glass, automobile tires, soap and toiletries, and pharmaceuticals. There is an automotive plant in Livingstone that assembles Isuzus and Peugeots. But the total working population of Zambia is very small, while the number of unemployed is growing rapidly.

Restrictions on foreigners, who often run many of the shops

and small businesses in other independent African countries, have kept the number of businesses small, and also have restricted the goods that are available. In the shops in Zambia, the shelves are nearly empty and there is little choice of brand or type of product.

FOREIGN INVESTMENT IN ZAMBIA

Because of the nationalization of foreign companies' properties and the restrictions on private ownership in industry, there has been little new investment in Zambia. One notable exception is the project created by an American-based firm, Lummus Agricultural Services Company. This Georgia-based firm specializes in making cotton gins, the machines that process cotton. Cotton grows well in Zambia, and there were four ginneries already working when Lummus began its project. According to Yosi Halevi, who directs the project in Zambia, his company established a branch dedicated to projects in Third World countries. "It's not enough for the developing countries to buy the machines. They want to get the technology of how to grow the cotton. Before, we used to only sell the gin; now we offer to customers the possibility to purchase the know-how. We design and implement the project. We have the experience how to do it. This is our first complete job."

What Lummus had to find in Zambia was the right combination of ingredients, and they found it at Lake Kariba. Halevi says, "It's a rare combination in Zambia: good soils and plenty of water, access roads, and not too far from electricity. In Zambia, electricity is cheap; they have more of an electrical grid than many Third World countries I have been in."

The farm is located in the Gwembe valley at the Sinazongwe

farm on Lake Kariba's north shore. It is about five thousand acres (two thousand hectares), and employs 250 permanent employees on the farm and ginnery. Another 1,000 people are employed for about six months of the year for weeding and harvesting. The workers include not only men and women, but children as well. This is typical for seasonal farm work all over the world. Even in the United States, seasonal workers are brought in to harvest the crops and there are often children working with their parents too.

Getting a large project such as this one started can sometimes get bogged down in development and Lummus wanted to be sure that did not happen in Zambia. "It took just one year from bush to the first crop," Halevi says, "and that is really quick. A project usually takes 10 years to develop and you lose the purpose and direction. We blitzed it. To have the money available, public money, the World Bank, it takes years to comply with requirements for the loans. We applied for this money but the day we applied, we started the project with our money. By the time the money came we were running. We took the risk ourselves. We had confidence in the project. It cost us money but we believe it was the only way to do it."

It will take years for the investment to pay back, but Lummus, which has been in business for 150 years, is confident about it. The restrictions on taking profits out of the country do not apply until the firm repays the World Bank loan. After that, Halevi says, "You can send 50 percent of your export proceeds out of the country." With the profits they cannot take out of the country, Lummus will invest in another project, one the company already is beginning to work on. Cotton is a cash crop for Zambia and is an important step in Zambia's search to develop export-earning products other than copper. By providing jobs, the farm also helps to keep more and more people from moving to the cities where there is not enough work.

But growing cotton only takes part of the year. When the cotton growing season is over, wheat is planted and grown for local consumption. This helps the economy too, since right now wheat must be imported. Cotton is one of Zambia's biggest success stories. The country produces all it needs for its own use and exports millions of pounds to other countries.

The cotton farm at Sinazongwe uses a system called center pivot irrigation that was developed in America. Instead of planting in long, straight rows, the crops are planted in huge circles. The irrigation arms are powered from the center of the circle. This method allows the farmer to control not only the water, but also fertilizer and insecticides, all of which are applied through the same system. This helps improve the yields. The system uses a lot of land, and in this area of Zambia there were people living on that land. The story of those people is very unusual.

THE KARIBA DAM

Before Zambia became independent, the big dam was built at Kariba. The dam created a new lake. The people who had been living on this land had to be moved away. These were the Tonga people. They were moved to an area just far enough away so that they would not be in the way of the lake. Now, thirty years later, the land these people were living on was given by the Zambian government to Lummus in order to start the cotton farm and the ginnery. Mr. Halevi says there were two small villages on the land, about sixty families in all. But Kevin Lowther, who works for Africare, an organization that helps refugees, worked with the people who were moved from this land. He says there were about six villages involved, with as many as three to four hundred families. "We were asked to come in after they had been moved off and work with them to get their own food production going." In a country as large as Zambia, with a relatively small population, why didn't Lummus look for empty land?

They could have found land without people, but not land that was suitable for agriculture. In the northeast, for example, up near the border with Tanzania, there is plenty of land that is uninhabited—but there is a good reason why no one lives there. Some of the land is swampy, and in other areas the soil is very poor. And for large-scale agricultural development, which requires a reliable source of clean water, this area is not suitable.

But agriculture is Zambia's great hope for the future. Zambia has the ability not only to feed its own people, but to earn foreign exchange from its food and other agricultural crops. And agriculture is the work that occupies more than 60 percent of Zambia's people.

AGRICULTURE

Although Zambia is a highly urbanized country, nearly two-thirds of its people continue to farm the land and live off their own produce. Agriculture is the country's great hope, the best chance it has to develop an economy that is not based on copper.

Only a small percent of Zambia's arable land is being farmed. Because the government has kept prices for farm products low, there has not been much incentive for the peasant farmers to increase their production. Most of the farming for profit is done by about twelve hundred large commercial farms, two-thirds of them run by Zambia's very small white population.

Above: A tea picker on a large commercial farm
Left: Plowing with oxen on a small farm

The rest are state farms or commercial farms run by Zambians. Although few in number, these large farms produce about 40 percent of the food and about 55 percent of the commercial crops. There are about 600,000 small-scale farmers. But they do not have the training, experience, or the money for equipment needed to run large commercial farms. Many of them, however, do produce a surplus, which they sell. President Kaunda declared that no person or group could own the land itself, so instead people use the land through hundred-year leases. All the land is owned by the state.

In some areas of the country, farmers practice a traditional form of slash-and-burn agriculture called *citemene*. It is intended to increase the soil fertility in areas where heavy rainfall often washes away nutrients. First the farmers set controlled fires in which they burn tree branches to nourish the soil. Then the land

73

Dried maize (right) is used for animal feed and also is ground into meal (left) and made into a thick porridge for human consumption.

is allowed to recover. Finally, various crops are planted. Cassava, a starchy vegetable, and millet are grown the first year, peanuts in the second year, and beans in the third. Farmers must be able to move off the land periodically to other areas while the land recovers from this three-year cycle. So far, there has been enough land to permit this, but with the population growing at such a fast rate, this system will become more and more difficult to sustain.

Just after independence, a major effort was made to introduce farm cooperatives. The idea was that these would increase agricultural output, in part by providing tractors to groups of farmers. Individual African farmers do not have machinery to help with their plowing and harvesting. Many cannot even afford a farm animal, such as an ox. But the bureaucracies that were set up to direct the companies only drained the economy. They did not create more food and other crops. The co-ops were abandoned by the early 1970s.

Most cattle are raised near the railroad in the south.

Although the country has a great farming potential, in the late 1980s it was still forced to import some food to make up for the shortfall in its own production. The basic food grown is maize (corn). This is often the main item in the people's diet. It is ground into a meal and eaten in the form of a thick porridge. Sometimes it is eaten whole as a vegetable. Maize also is grown as feed for farm animals, including poultry, beef cattle, and hogs. But as people moved to the cities, their diets changed. Pounding maize gave way to buying ready-made food such as bread. To cater to this growing taste for bread, farmers have begun to grow wheat. They have a long way to go to supply all the wheat that Zambia uses and must import wheat to make up for this shortage.

There are about two million head of cattle in Zambia, most of them within a short distance of the railroad in the southern part of Zambia. Both commercial and small farmers keep beef cattle and dairy herds, but the African farmers do not have access to cattle dips, baths in which a solution is applied to the cattle to keep them free of insects. Without the dips, insects such as tsetse flies infect the cattle and cause diseases.

The commercial farmers can afford to maintain their own dips. But the small farmer must rely on the government for this service, and the government has not been able to provide funds for dips. Zambians, like people in other African countries, like to keep cattle as a form of wealth. Cattle are slaughtered for important occasions such as weddings and funerals, but not as a regular source of food for the family. Zambians do not have a tradition of eating meat regularly.

A number of private companies have come into Zambia to participate in plans to grow wheat, maize, coffee, tobacco, and soybeans. One such project is at Mukumpu near the Copperbelt, where a variety of crops are being grown, and at Mpongwe, where wheat is being grown. Irrigation is the key to these projects, but the pumps that are vital to the irrigation run on either fuel oil or electricity. Small-scale farmers often do not have the knowledge to use proper irrigation and cannot afford to buy the materials for the system or the power to run it.

Sugar is produced from sugarcane grown at Mazabuka in Southern Province, near the Kafue River. The processing plant, located right in the middle of the sugar plantations, meets Zambia's total needs. Sugar also is used to make jams with fruits grown locally. A pineapple plantation in the Northwestern Province has its own processing plant and cannery now. Zambia has developed its sugar industry so well that it now supplies all its own needs and exports the surplus. The Curray Farm Ltd. is a major producer of peaches, which are grown during the European off-season and then air shipped directly to market. Peaches are

Clockwise from far left: A worker in a sugarcane field, a sunflower, and sunflower seeds

picked in Zambia one day, flown overnight to London, and are in the market the next morning. Rice and sunflower seeds are produced locally. The seeds are used to produce oil.

Kalangwa Estates, part of the huge Lonrho Zambia enterprises, produces onions and potatoes that are exported to neighboring countries.

FORESTRY

Just over half of the land in Zambia is forested. Some of this has been used to provide timber for the mines. The timber helps to hold up the shafts as the earth is removed from the mine. Wood is used also as fuel for cooking fires. Some exotic woods, such as teak, grow in southwestern Zambia and are harvested for use in hardwood floors, furniture, and prefabricated housing.

Fishermen on Lake Kariba

FISHING

About fifty thousand people are engaged in fishing in Zambia.
From their income they support about a quarter million people.
Many of them are commercial fishermen, while others fish only to
feed their own families. They fish the many lakes as well as the
floodplains of the rivers—and even the swamps. Lake Kariba, the
huge man-made lake that forms part of Zambia's border with
Zimbabwe, was stocked with fish and provides good fishing both
for food and for sport.

TRANSPORTATION: ZAMBIA'S RAILROADS

Cecil Rhodes's dream of a Cape-to-Cairo railroad very nearly
became a reality. After the First World War, all the territories
between Cape Town, South Africa, and Cairo, Egypt, running

along the eastern part of Africa had ties to England and might have been linked up with a railway system. Thanks to that dream, the railway system was well developed in Zambia long before there were either goods to carry or many people to ride on it. Today, the railroads permit easy travel to all the main cities of Zambia. They also connect the country with the ports of the neighboring countries.

The railroad shaped the development of the country while providing transport for the copper. All the towns on the Copperbelt, as well as virtually all the towns of any importance in Zambia, are situated along the railroad. Forty percent of the people live within twenty-nine miles (forty kilometers) of a rail line. Much of the cattle in Zambia is raised along the rail line, which makes it easy to transport the animals to market. The railroads are crucial to the economy of Zambia, since the landlocked country has no ports of its own.

The main line starts at Livingstone on the southern border of Zambia and heads northeast to Lusaka, the capital, and then straight north up to the Copperbelt. This was the original rail line, built between 1905 and 1909. It runs for 684 miles (1,100 kilometers), including the branches within the Copperbelt and in the forest logging area. At the northern border of Zambia, the line connects with Zaire's railway system. From Livingstone, the rail line crosses a bridge into Zimbabwe. Goods travel south along Zimbabwe's railroad and ultimately out through ports on the Indian Ocean.

Most of the goods still go through South African ports although both Zimbabwe and Zambia would prefer not to have to do any business with South Africa. They would rather use the line that runs from Zimbabwe through Mozambique, but the civil war in

Mozambique has made this impossible. Recently, however, a corridor was created to protect this line and Zambia has begun to move its goods out along this corridor to the port of Beira in Mozambique. The Beira Corridor is the shortest distance that goods from Zambia can travel to reach a port. But it is still a very long trip and right now can only carry a small percent of Zambia's production.

The second rail line, about 530 miles (860 kilometers) long, is the Tan-Zam or Tazara line. It runs northeast from Kapiri Mposhi up to the Tanzania border and then continues through Tanzania to the port city of Dar es Salaam. The need for this line became desperate in the 1960s after the border between Zambia and Southern Rhodesia was closed. The Zambians would prefer to use the port at Dar es Salaam instead of those in South Africa, but it is not very efficient or reliable. Goods sent to Dar es Salaam often wait a long time before they can be put on ships. It can take three weeks or three months before something reaches Zambia from the port. So even though Tanzania is a country that shares the same belief in socialism as Zambia, when it comes to the economy, the Zambians are forced to take their business elsewhere. Goods from southern Zaire are shipped out through Zambia, adding to the importance of the rail lines.

There is another rail line that is important to Zambia—the Benguela railroad in Angola. This line runs from Angola's port city of Benguela, across the country and into Zaire, connecting up with Zambia's rail line at the border between the two countries. The Benguela has been the victim of the civil war that has raged in Angola for more than ten years. Zambia hopes that a protected strip of land, similar to that in Mozambique, will open up this line again. It would be called the Lobito Corridor and would provide another outlet for Zambia's copper. Before it closed in 1975, the Benguela carried one-third of Zambia's copper exports.

Zambia's railroads have been modernized and no longer use steam except for shunting operations. But some of the old steam trains can be seen at the Railway Museum in Livingstone. This was established at the site of the old Zambezi Saw Mills Railway line. And visitors can even take mini train rides here on trains pulled by old steam locomotives.

TOURISM

One of the brightest hopes for the economy in Zambia is in the area of tourism. The pleasant climate adds to the pleasures of visiting Zambia's game parks and other tourist areas. The country has not been discovered in the way East Africa has, so there are fewer visitors. This makes it a more natural experience. There are many areas of Zambia that have been set aside as game reserves, but not all of them are ready for visitors. In the future, the country hopes that increasing numbers of tourists will enable them to create lodges and campsites in these areas as well.

In 1988, Zambia Airways introduced a direct flight from New York City to Lusaka. This fourteen-hour trip takes the visitor to the heart of Africa without spending two days to get there. The plane stops for refueling in Monrovia, Liberia, on the west coast of Africa before proceeding to Zambia. To inaugurate the flight, a special reception was held in New York, where ceremonial drummers and cultural dancers entertained the guests. In attendance were three of Zambia's cabinet ministers, including the minister of tourism.

The best-known tourist attraction in Zambia is Victoria Falls, on

The breathtaking beauty of Victoria Falls

the Zambezi River. Here, visitors can experience mosi ao tunya, the smoke that thunders. They feel the same wonder that overcame David Livingstone when he saw the falls and named them for Queen Victoria of Great Britain. The roar of the falls varies during the year, rising during the rainy season, and then falling during the dry months. When the flow of the Zambezi is at its peak, the volume of water going over the falls is at its highest: 75 million gallons (284 million liters) pass over the mile-wide falls every minute, then drop 348 feet (106 meters) to join the Zambezi River as it continues its flow.

It is actually better to see the falls when the water volume is not quite so high, and the mist does not obscure the view of Zimbabwe on the other side. At this time of the year, many of the Europeans who live in Zambia and the neighboring countries, as well as visitors from abroad, enjoy river rafting trips. The trips begin at Rainbow Lodge in Livingstone, just a short walk from the

A rafting boat on the Zambezi River

river. Running along the lower portion of the river, the rubber
boats take eight people at a time on a wild ride through the steep
canyons. There is scarcely time to enjoy the beautiful scenery as
the passengers paddle as hard as they can to keep the boat
upright. There are also boat trips on calmer portions of the river,
where the tourist can watch for animals along the shore, or pass
some hippos right in the water, their huge bodies mostly
submerged.

Less strenuous is a visit to Luangwa Valley National Park,
known for its great herds of elephants. This huge park, 3,475
square miles (9,000 square kilometers), is 458 miles (737 kilometers)
from Lusaka. It has one of the largest concentrations of wildlife
remaining in Africa. And here visitors can experience the wildlife
in the most extraordinary way—on foot. Norman Carr, who has
lived in the Zambian bush all his life, is known as the father of the
walking safari. His knowledge of the animals' habits encouraged

Guided walking safaris in the national parks are an exciting way to see and photograph animals and birds.

him to begin trips that take people for long walks right through the park. The Zambia government likes the idea of letting people have a very natural experience.

The largest game reserve in Zambia is Kafue National Park, 8,687 square miles (22,500 square kilometers) — less than an hour's flight from Lusaka. This park is half the size of Switzerland. Guided walking safaris here begin at the camps and take visitors roaming among the animals. They also travel by Land Rover from one area to the next. The season runs from June through October. After that the rains make many roads within the park impassable.

POACHING

The huge size of these parks is a big advantage to poachers, people who kill the animals and sell their skins, tusks, and horns, which is against the law and also is a threat to the animals' continued existence. It is not possible to have enough park rangers

Lions, zebras, and giraffes are just a few of the animals to be seen in Zambia's national parks.

to patrol these enormous stretches of land, so the poachers have been very successful in their illegal activities. They have just about wiped out the rhinoceroses in Zambia.

The situation in terms of the elephant is rapidly becoming just as desperate. In the late 1970s, there were an estimated 100,000 elephants in the Luangwa valley. Today, there are about a quarter of that number, and every day more of them are killed and the valuable ivory is smuggled out to Hong Kong and southwest Asia where it is carved and offered for sale. The Zambia government needs all the help it can get, because it cannot afford the money for the park rangers or the vehicles needed to patrol the parks.

To help Zambians understand the need for animal conservation, special clubs were set up for the schoolchildren. Called Chongologo Clubs, they have about forty thousand members between the ages of seven and fourteen. There is also a similar club for older students in secondary schools and colleges, with more than five thousand students enrolled.

Kariba Dam and its lake on the Zambezi River

LAKE KARIBA

When the Zambezi River was dammed to create electrical
energy for the Federation, it also created an enormous lake,
Kariba. The lake is 20 miles (32 kilometers) wide by 170 miles
(274 kilometers) long, and sets the scene for a variety of water
activities enjoyed by tourists and by local people as well. Fishing
is one of the major activities here. The annual tiger fish contest
attracts entrants from all over the world. Giant catfish, eel, and

Left: Wind surfing on Lake Kariba
Right: Partially submerged hippos in the water

many other species are there for the catching also. Wind surfing is one of the most popular sports enjoyed at Kariba.

During Zimbabwe's war for independence, areas along the Zambian side of the lake were shelled. Now, with peace in Zimbabwe, this area is being developed for tourism and for local people who are building weekend cottages.

The dam itself is a popular tourist site with its massive curved cement wall that holds back 400 million pounds (181 million kilograms) of water. The dam wall is as tall as a forty-story building and has a roadway on the top that permits visitors to drive their cars along for a spectacular view.

Fishing is also popular at Lake Tanganyika, at the extreme northeast corner of Zambia. Here, Nile perch, weighing up to 130 pounds (59 kilograms), and giant catfish, up to 200 pounds (91 kilograms), give fishermen a really vigorous workout. Visitors must be careful of the hippos in the lake; they might just bump into the boat and turn the fishermen into swimmers.

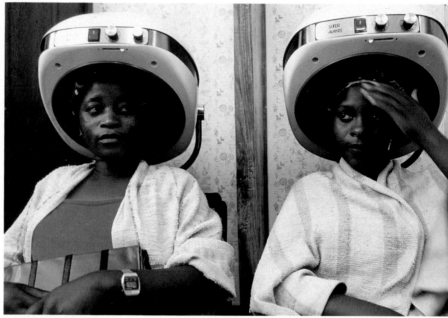

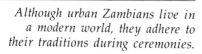
Although urban Zambians live in a modern world, they adhere to their traditions during ceremonies.

Chapter 6

EVERYDAY LIFE

THE PEOPLE

Zambia's population of over seven million people is quite small when measured against the size of the country, but the figures by themselves tell only part of the story. About 45 percent of the people live in the urban areas, a very high percentage for black Africa. Most of them live in Lusaka or around the cities of the Copperbelt. That uneven distribution reflects the country's historical economic dependence on copper. The copper mines have been the central attraction for men seeking work in Zambia for more than fifty years. Since the railroads were built to export the copper, the population became centered around the rail line. Only three of the country's towns of any size—Lusaka, Kabwe, and Livingstone—are located outside the Copperbelt. About one million people live in Lusaka, the capital. Three of the major Copperbelt cities are Kitwe and Ndola, each with more than 400,000 people, and Chingola, with about 250,000. The birthrate in Zambia is very high and the population has doubled since independence.

When the demand for Zambia's copper fell, many of the workers were dismissed. There were no other jobs for them to take and yet they could not build new lives in the countryside. Many of them had lived in the Copperbelt their whole lives. They didn't know how to live on the land and farm like the people in the farming areas.

As people moved to the cities, they became less and less attached to their traditional life and the traditional lands. In Africa, land is not "owned" in the Western sense. The people have a right to live on the land because their parents and grandparents lived there. But when they move away, they give up this right and they also give up a kinship with the rest of the people who remain behind. They are said to be "detribalized."

When the people live in such an area, they are under the rule of their own chief. He listens to complaints, settles disputes, and punishes anyone found guilty of breaking their law. But when the people move to the cities and towns, they no longer have a chief to look after them. They become subject to civil law. Their loyalty is given to their own family and it is the family that is responsible for its own needs. This lack of an overall authority gave birth to the regional self-help societies that sprang up in the years before independence. These organizations tried to take the place of the system of chieftainship, to give people a group that it could turn to in time of need. They were the first political organizations in Zambia and were crucial in the fight for independence.

PEOPLE AND LANGUAGES

Unlike many other central African countries, no single cultural group dominates the population. With more than seventy recognized ethnic groups and as many as eighty different languages, the people have accepted English as the official language. This holdover from the days when Zambia was a British colony offers a neutral language that does not give one cultural group preference over another. There are four major cultural groupings in Zambia. The Bemba live mainly in the north. The Lunda are in the northeast. The Lozi are dominant in the west, in the area that used to be called Barotseland. In the east are the Ngoni. Each group migrated into the area now known as Zambia from neighboring territories, but all had arrived before the first missionaries came to the land. Three of the four groups, the Lozi, Bemba, and Lunda, migrated from the Congo Basin (now part of Zaire). The Lozi came into Zambia in the seventeenth century. The Bemba followed them about one hundred years later, in the beginning of the eighteenth century. The Lunda came at about the same time as the Bemba, or just after. The Ngoni are a branch of the Zulu people who were driven out of the land that is now part of South Africa by Shaka, the Zulu king, around 1820. The Tonga and other small cultural groups live in the south, around Lake Kariba.

Bemba is the most widely spoken language in Zambia. Because the Bemba live in the north, the Copperbelt area where the population is the most concentrated, it was natural for other people coming to the area to learn the language. In addition, a dialect of Bemba is the language used in the mines. It allows the mine workers from different language groups to understand each other. Although English is the official language of Zambia, it is spoken mainly by educated people, in business and in government. People who do not come into contact with officials or who do not live in the cities have little use for English and speak their own language. Many people in Zambia speak both their own ethnic language and English. To promote the concept of a united Zambia, President Kaunda speaks in English in all his public appearances.

The kuomoboka

CHIEFS

The role of the chief in Zambia varies greatly. Among the Lozi, the paramount chief, called the *litunga,* is a greatly revered figure. Each year, as the Zambezi River rises with the new rains, the plains where the litunga lives begin to flood. As the water rises, the litunga and his entire court move to high land in a grand ceremony called the *kuomoboka.* A long, specially designed royal barge, with forty oarsmen, carefully transports the chief to safety. Another barge carries the royal drummers who play all along the trip. All the others travel along as well in their own, simple dugout canoes. In the fall, the whole trip is reversed as the litunga returns to his traditional home.

Among the Tonga, however, there are no chiefs who are recognized as leaders. The Tonga lived in household groups, not villages. Their name, *Tonga,* comes from a Shona word meaning

The skyline of Lusaka

"independent." They have cultural ties, but not political ones. The Tonga did not even think of themselves as a distinct culture until the British colonial officials apppointed chiefs over them and gave them a recognized identity.

The most visible remnant of the system of chiefs is the House of Chiefs, an advisory group that meets only a few days a year. It advises the government on matters that affect the traditional leaders and their people, but it does not have the power to make law. There are twenty-seven members, representing all the provinces.

LUSAKA, THE CAPITAL

The population of the capital city has reached one million, including the squatter communities that encircle it, but Lusaka still has the feel of a small town. The occasional tractor can be

Lusaka

Left: The National Assembly Building
Above: A view of Lusaka from the
northern end of Cairo Road.

seen rolling down its main street, Cairo Road, named for the long
dreamed of Cape-to-Cairo railroad. Lusaka houses the national
government as well as the University of Zambia and the National
Archives. It is also home to the high commissions and foreign
embassies including that of the United States and the U.S.S.R.
There is a five-star hotel here, the Pamodzi, the most popular
meeting place for diplomats, as well as foreign and local
businessmen. Local cinemas show films mostly from the United
States. The popular, violence-filled kung fu films from Hong Kong
and Taiwan were banned by President Kaunda because they were
influencing young people to form gangs. Now, ninja movies, and
ninja gangs, have taken their place.

Hotel Pamodzi (left) and the Lusaka market

The Pamodzi, as well as the embassies, are located a few miles from the center of Lusaka, out in the green belt. The feeling of country is never far away in Zambia.

In town, there are offices catering to tourists, including a number of organizations that will book visitors on hunting safaris. Controlled hunting, with a license required for each animal shot, is considered a good way to raise funds for the country and to keep a close eye on the people who hunt for sport. It also puts a few more licensed people out in the bush to prevent the poachers from killing animals indiscriminately.

Curio shops that sell souvenirs made of copper have to import the finished products from England. Zambia does not have facilities to turn its own copper into clocks, plaques, and planters.

*A billboard calls
President Kaunda
"Father of the Nation."*

OTHER CITIES

Ndola, a Copperbelt town, is the major industrial city in the north. It is a sprawling city, with attractive buildings and tree-lined streets. Many companies have headquarters here, offshoots of the copper mining industry. It is an administrative, commercial, and transportation center as well. The oil pipeline from Dar es Salaam ends here. The *Times of Zambia* is printed in Ndola and every July the town hosts an international trade fair.

Kitwe is the biggest town in the Copperbelt, with more than 300,000 people. It is the site of Nkana, the deepest copper mine in Zambia. The mine produces 200,000 tons (90 million kilograms) of copper a year. The town also has a refinery and the Copperbelt Museum. The Zambia Institute of Technology offers technical courses, while the College of Applied Arts and Commerce focuses on commercial subjects. The weather here is much warmer than in Lusaka.

Livingstone is a popular tourist town near Victoria Falls. It was the first capital of Northern Rhodesia. It has a population of about 75,000, and offers an appealing, old-fashioned look at the way the country appeared in the past. It is the home of the Livingstone Museum and also has fine tourist facilities.

RELIGION

The arrival of white missionaries in Zambia in the nineteenth century brought Western religion to the people. From the start, the church was associated with learning and modern ideas, since the only schools that were open to the Africans were those run by missionaries. This continued until independence, making a very strong connection between knowledge and religion. The church also offered the only chance for an African to achieve social standing and respect in the new community as well as a responsible position.

Before the missionaries arrived, there was a rich tradition of spirits living among the people. Those who had just died were still considered part of the family and demanded respect. Decisions that were made by the living had to be made known to these spirits, who could help their descendants. If ignored, however, the spirits might become angry and could harm the family through supernatural power. Part of the system for dealing with the power of bad spirits involved the use of herbal remedies, which is then tied in with healing.

Most Zambians continue to keep in contact with their traditional belief systems. They find a way to maintain both traditional beliefs and to practice Christianity. Right from the start, the missionaries tried to prevent the people they were converting from continuing to believe in traditional religion, but

Many Zambians practice Christianity (left), while still maintaining their traditional beliefs, personified by the medicine man at the right.

they were not very successful. In modern times, the Catholic church had to deal with the African bishop of Lusaka who was practicing a kind of healing that the church called "witchcraft." He was summoned back to Rome by the pope and has been kept there, away from the people who look to him for spiritual guidance. Among some groups, where there is not a strong tradition of chiefs, religious figures such as prophets and rain priests served as the only authorities. They often acted as courts, determining who was guilty and who was innocent. Among the Lozi, the king was thought to have descended directly from God.

Since independence, with the state taking over the responsibility of primary education, the churches no longer have the same kind of direct influence they once had. It is estimated, however, that about half of the population considers itself to be Christian, the majority of them Roman Catholic.

The annual salute to youth, a new ritual,
is celebrated as an official holiday in March.

RITUALS

Initiation ceremonies for boys and girls vary from one culture to another, but usually take place around the time of puberty. Instruction in how to behave as wives is an important part of the girls' ceremony. They are instructed in sex, marriage, how to bring up children, and the values of the culture.

For boys, initiation ceremonies usually involve circumcision. The boys are taught the important aspects of life that pertain to them—hunting, understanding nature, and the lore of the culture.

Bride-price, called *lobola*, is paid by the man to the bride's father. Traditionally, lobola was paid in cattle. For those who did not keep cattle, payment was in the form of services performed by the groom. Today, bride-price is often determined by the level of education the girl has achieved. This payment is a form of insurance, meant to protect the bride from being badly treated by her husband. It must be returned to the husband's family if the wife finds cause to leave him.

Musicians playing a unique form of xylophone (left) and drums (right)

MUSIC AND DANCE

Traditional dancing, accompanied by drums and other instruments, is the most enduring aspect of African culture in Zambia. At all important occasions, ceremonial drummers are present to greet the arrival of dignitaries. In addition to drums, the hand piano and the xylophone are popular instruments. All the instruments are made locally of skins, metal strips, and wood.

Dances are performed by lines of dancers, men in one row, women in another. Many dances depict important cultural occasions, such as a puberty rite. Music and dance combine in rituals that symbolize the casting out of spirit demons. It is believed that the gods may be approached through special pieces of music. Contemporary music has become part of the social scene in Zambia, especially musical styles and instruments from neighboring African countries.

A sampling of Zambian crafts includes intricate basketwork (top left), a carved wooden statue wearing a costume made of beads (center), a mask of bark and mud (right), and wooden animals for sale by the young men who carved them (left).

ART

Mask making is the special art of the people of the Northwestern Province. Using bark and mud, these masks are made into ferocious faces and painted in black, white, and red.

Handicrafts are usually confined to practical, everyday objects, such as animal traps, pottery, and sleeping masks. There is some decorative beadwork, and basket making, as well as weaving of *chitenges*, brightly colored cloths that are wrapped around the body and worn as the national dress. Wooden sculptures are carved by men and may often be seen around tourist sites such as at Livingstone. Here, visitors can purchase these charming figures directly from the men who carve them.

Boys playing soccer

While painting is not one of the arts of Zambia today, rock paintings from the Stone Age reveal the life of the ancient people who lived here. Animals and people are shown, often in hunting scenes. Some rock paintings may still be seen at Mwelwa in the Northern Province.

SPORTS

Like many countries around the world, soccer is the most popular sport in Zambia. A national soccer team went to the Olympics held in South Korea in 1988.

A Zambian boxer won a bronze medal in the lightweight division at the 1984 Olympics.

Other popular sports include badminton, squash, baseball, and rugby. Golf, very expensive for participants, is considered a very prestigious sport in Zambia. While boys like to play soccer, girls prefer netball, which Americans call basketball.

EDUCATION

It takes educated people to run a country. Yet when Kenneth Kaunda became president of Zambia, there were just one hundred college graduates and about twelve thousand who had completed high school. It was estimated that no more than 3 percent of the entire population had completed primary school. The British, during their colonial administration of the territory, had given little thought to educating the people whose lives they controlled. That was left to the missionaries. It was in a missionary school in Nyasaland (now Malawi) that President Kaunda received his early education. There was not one university in the entire country. Anyone who reached that level had to go to another country to continue studying. Many went to college in Southern Rhodesia, which had some facilities that were built during the period of Federation.

Improving the educational standards was one of the first tasks the president set for the country after independence. He put as much money into building up the school system as he could, and within seven years the number of children in elementary school had doubled. It was difficult to tackle the problem all at once, since there were not enough schoolrooms, supplies, and especially, teachers. Foreign teachers came to Zambia to teach while the country trained its own teachers.

The crash program designed to bring the level of education up to a reasonable standard was hit hard, like everything else in Zambia, when sanctions were declared against Southern Rhodesia. Money that would have gone to the schools had to be used to defend the country, and to build roads and a railroad.

At the same time, the number of schoolchildren was increasing

This woman continued her education past the primary level.

dramatically. Today, nearly half of Zambia's seven million people are under the age of fifteen. Most of them drop out of school when they complete the elementary grades. Yet many do not even get past the fourth grade, not long enough to attain proficiency in English. Many of the teachers in the primary grades have only a primary education themselves.

For those who do go on, two exams separate them and decide the paths they will follow. The first, given at eighth-grade level, determines whether or not a student will go on to high school. At the tenth grade, another exam determines how many will go on to the last years of high school. Because there are so few places available in high school, the passing grade is kept very high and very few are able to complete high school. In 1964, only 14,000 students attended secondary schools. In the 1980s, there were 115,000, still far fewer than the number of young people who should be in school. There are a number of technical training schools offering practical instruction that will help the students find jobs, which are even more scarce in Zambia than there are places in school.

The lack of spaces becomes even more desperate for those who want to go on to a university. Zambia University was opened in 1966, but it only has room for a few thousand students of all those who would like to attend. Even very bright students find themselves shut out. Their only hope is to be invited by some organization to attend college in another country.

For students of any age, and for adults as well, there is a serious shortage of books available to read. The problem, once again, is the lack of foreign exchange with which to buy books. President Kaunda says the population is getting "only rubbish." All the book dealers can afford to import is inexpensive, popular works. They will not put their allowance of money into less popular, more expensive reading material. A foundation has been established to create a book program but, while foreign exchange remains a problem, its success must be limited.

HEALTH

Zambia suffers from most of central Africa's major health threats. It has a high infection rate from diseases associated with impure water. Few people have access to safe, pure drinking water. They use the rivers, which are often breeding sites for insects that carry disease. One of the most devastating diseases in Zambia is river blindness caused by the bite of an infected black fly. This is most often found in the swamplands of Luapula Province. A vaccine has been developed to prevent this disease and is now being used in parts of West Africa. In time it is hoped it will become available to Zambia as well.

Malaria, which is carried by mosquitos, causes very high fevers and sometimes death and is widespread in Zambia, especially in

Zambia has a high infant mortality rate.

the Northern Province, with its swampy areas. There are drugs that can prevent malaria, or at least weaken its impact, and these always are used by visitors to the country, and often by the European community as well. But for the general population, these drugs are expensive and not widely available. Sleeping sickness, carried by the tsetse fly, is restricted to certain areas of the country, but is usually fatal. It affects cattle as well as people.

Zambia has a very high infant mortality rate, often caused by dysentery. This is brought about by water infected with disease. Measles, now occasionally known in Western countries, is still common in Zambia and frequently causes death. Childhood illnesses are often made worse by malnutrition, which causes Zambia to have a high death rate for children under the age of five. It is caused by a diet that is often limited to maize meal, which is starchy and does not supply any protein. Cassava, another staple of the diet, is also starchy and provides almost no nutrition at all. It simply fills an empty stomach. The life expectancy at birth is fifty-two years. Women live slightly longer than men. Only 4 percent of the people are over sixty years old.

It is difficult for Zambians to get good health care. In the countryside, there are few health clinics and the people live so far apart they often cannot get to the clinics that do exist. The government was working hard to bring health clinics to more people, but the lack of funds has made it difficult to carry out these programs. There are not enough doctors in Zambia to take care of the people. Often, in the smaller regional hospitals, nurses and medical assistants provide nearly all the health services that are offered, with a doctor supervising.

In addition to Western health care, Zambians sometimes turn to traditional medicine, such as herbal treatments. Many of these same herbs are used, in more standardized form, by Western physicians. Many drugs are derived from natural ingredients that are found growing wild.

In addition to traditional health problems, Zambia suffers greatly from AIDS. Unlike some other places, AIDS in Africa affects men and women equally. It is spread by a person carrying the disease through normal, heterosexual intercourse. There is a higher incidence of AIDS in the urban areas where people from outside the area bring the disease in with them. It is believed that AIDS originated in Zaire, just across the border, and this makes it a very controversial subject.

Since President Kaunda revealed that one of his sons died from AIDS in 1987, in Zambia at least it has become more openly discussed. There is still no known cure, although people have received education in how to prevent the illness by using contraceptive devices. However, there is still a lack of acceptance that the disease is spread by sexual contact and can be prevented. The Zambian government, funded by the World Health Organization, has embarked on a five-year plan to fight AIDS.

A rural Zambian family outside their house

Zambia has one of the highest birthrates in the world. The population has doubled between 1964 and 1988. Yet with the very high rate of infant and child deaths, people are still concerned to have many children in order to ensure that enough will live. Birth control is not much of an issue in Zambia and even for those who wish to practice it, the cost for birth control devices, such as condoms, is extremely high.

Another of Zambia's major health problems is alcoholism. In the rural areas, people brew their own beer, which has a low alcohol content. There, it is used as part of ceremonies and rituals. But when people move to the urban areas, they buy commercial beer, which is much more intoxicating. President Kaunda, who does not drink any alcoholic beverages, has been very active in the campaign to reduce alcoholism in Zambia.

Chapter 7

ZAMBIA AND
THE WORLD

WELCOMING REFUGEES

Zambia's location and the policy of its leader has made it the temporary home of refugees from many countries. It borders on countries in which civil wars have been raging for many years. Many people have been forced to leave their homes, and sometimes their countries as well, in order to escape the fighting. President Kaunda believes it is the duty of Zambia and its people to provide a refuge for these neighbors, and to assist them until they can return home. From Angola, people flee over the border into western Zambia. From Mozambique, people escape into eastern Zambia. All of them need shelter, food, and medical care.

Zambia also has been the home of those who need a base from which to plan how to end the problems in their own countries. Before Zimbabwe became independent, Zambia provided shelter for one of the groups fighting against white rule. And South African resistance groups find a home in Zambia as well. These people make Zambia a target for attacks, but President Kaunda believes that it is his duty to help his neighbors. In fact, the

Zambian government's support for liberation fronts is written into the national constitution.

There are about 140,000 refugees in Zambia. One-third have arrived since 1986. Most, almost 100,000, come from Angola, and another 28,000 come from Mozambique. Nine thousand are from Zaire, 6,500 from Namibia, and 3,500 from South Africa. The South Africans are virtually all members of the ANC, fighting to gain black majority rule in South Africa. While most of the other refugees are peasant farmers who settle in the rural areas, the ANC refugees all live in and around Lusaka.

A group that helps Zambia to carry out this humanitarian work is Africare. Kevin Lowther worked in Zambia for five years, helping to settle Angolans who escaped into Zambia's Northwest Province. "We first provided basic foods and agricultural assistance for the Nehaba refugee settlement there. We also helped assist Mozambicans who came into the Eastern Province. Zambia has been a convenient area for refugees because of its central location. Some of them will never go back. There are probably close to 100,000 that are spontaneously settled. Some refugees have been in Zambia 15 to 20 years. When you have kids born and raised in a new country, it's difficult to go back."

Many of these people are of the same culture as the people in Zambia. The concept of a nation is less important to them than their loyalty to the people with whom they share the same language and cultures. When they find people who do share these things, it is not as difficult to stay. For many, Zambia provides the only peace they have known.

Africare has been working in Zambia for ten years, working to help the country revive its own agriculture, not only in refugee areas, but for the general population as well. Three years of

A meeting of delegates from the Front-Line States

drought in the 1980s, plus bad planning, forced Zambia to import food. Lowther says, "The country is finally getting itself back to the point of growing all its own food. Maize is the principal crop. Now they're diversifying into sorghum and millet for home use and growing soybeans on a commercial basis."

ZAMBIA'S PLACE IN THE WORLD

President Kaunda has been a forceful presence in the world community since taking office in 1964. He has twice been named chairman of the Organization of African Unity (OAU), in 1973 and again in 1987. From 1970 through 1973, he was president of the Non-aligned Nations. He is also chairman of the Front-Line States, the countries that border South Africa and are most directly affected by the continuation of its system of racial separation called apartheid. On October 26, 1988, he was reelected president of Zambia by an overwhelming majority—running unopposed as Zambia is a one-party state.

As OAU chairman, President Kaunda addressed the United Nations about Africa and the United Nations' program for African economic recovery and development. He said, "That program is a unique framework for cooperation between Africa and the international community to bring about Africa's economic recovery. We have introduced painful economic reforms, often at tremendous economic and social cost and at risk of political stability. All of this was taking place during drought conditions. South Africa's policies have demanded financial and human cost and undermined peace and stability. In spite of all this, Africa has demonstrated its unswerving commitment to UN economic recovery program." But the results have been disheartening, he added: "Africa lost as much as $19 billion in exports and the purchasing power of its exports fell to 30 percent. Debt has assumed alarming dimensions."

In fact, Africa's debts exceed its export earnings four times over and Zambia is one of the countries that is overwhelmed by its debt. Late in 1987, President Kaunda declared that Zambia was no longer able to comply with the demands of the International Monetary Fund (IMF). The IMF set certain requirements in order for Zambia to continue to receive new loans. But these requirements, such as higher food prices, caused food riots in Zambia and left fifteen people dead. The many people out of work in the Copperbelt cannot afford to pay more for maize. While President Kaunda tries to stand up to South Africa and comply with sanctions, the people in his own country do not have enough money to buy food. He has to decide whether to make a short-term decision that will satisfy people today and not worry about tomorrow, or to take unpopular steps in order to plan for a better future.

Maize (left), being stacked for shipment, is Zambia's basic food crop and copper (above) is Zambia's chief export.

Many of the other countries in Africa suffer some of the same problems as Zambia. They decided to band together to find a way to ease their economic difficulties and to get around the problems of foreign exchange. These nine countries—Zambia, Zimbabwe, Botswana, Angola, Mozambique, Malawi, Swaziland, Tanzania, and Lesotho—formed an organization called the Southern African Development Coordination Conference (SADCC). The idea is to be able to barter for goods from one country to another, eliminating cash and trade barriers from transactions. One country has wheat, another has manufacturing services, and they exchange them on an even basis. Each country has an economic area that it coordinates, according to its own resources. Although SADCC was formed in 1980, it is only beginning to see significant results. But there are great hopes that in the future it will have a positive impact on the economies of southern Africa. It is also a way for these countries to avoid dealing with South Africa, the strongest economic force in all of black Africa.

114

MINI-FACTS AT A GLANCE

GENERAL INFORMATION

Official Name: Republic of Zambia

Capital: Lusaka

Official Language: English (spoken by educated people, in business and in government). Bemba, however, is the most widely spoken language.

Government: Zambia is an independent one-party republic. Executive power under the 1973 constitution is vested in the president, who is elected to a five-year term. The prime minister and other Cabinet officers are chosen from the National Assembly by the president.
    The only political party is the United National Independence party (UNIP).
    The highest court is the Supreme Court; below it are the High Court, the Magisterial Court, and the local courts. Law is based on the English common law.

National Anthem: Zambia National Anthem (First line: "Stand and sing of Zambia, proud and free")

Flag: Three vertical stripes—red for freedom, black for the people, orange for mineral wealth—on a field of green for natural resources. There is an orange eagle in the upper-right corner.

Money: The basic unit of currency is the kwacha. In 1986 there were 6.99 kwacha to one U.S. dollar.

Weights and Measures: The metric system is used.

Population: 6,800,000 (1987-88 estimate); 51 percent rural, 49 percent urban

Major Cities:

Lusaka	818,994
Kitwe	449,442
Ndola	418,142
Chingola	187,310
Luanshya	168,167

(Population based on mid-1987 estimate.)

Religion: It is estimated that about half of the population considers itself to be Christian, the majority of them Roman Catholic. Traditional beliefs still have a strong hold on the people, however, even on those who practice Christianity.

GEOGRAPHY

Highest point: 7,123 ft. (2,171 m) on the Nyika Plateau

Lowest point: At the confluence of the Zambezi and Luangwa rivers, 1,500 ft. (361 m) above sea level

Mountains: The Muchinga Mountains in the northeast rise to a height of 7,000 ft. (2,100 m). Other high elevations are the Mbala Plateau (5,000 to 6,000 ft.; 1,524 to 1,828 m) in the north and the Mafingi Mountains in the northeast.

Rivers: The Zambezi flows south through the western part of the country. It was first explored by David Livingstone. The Zambezi separates Zambia from Namibia, Botswana, and Zimbabwe. There are three main tributary systems: those of the Kafue, Luangwa, and Lusemfwa rivers.

Climate: The altitude gives Zambia a milder climate than one would expect. The hot season lasts from September through November, when the temperature at midday ranges from 80 to 100° F. (27 to 38° C). There is a rainy season from November to April, and there are floods and violent storms in March. From May through August temperatures range from 60 to 80° F. (16 to 27° C).
Northern Zambia gets about 50 in. (130 cm) of rain per year; southern, 20 to 30 in. (51 to 76 cm).

Greatest Distances: East to west: 900 mi. (1,448 km)
North to south: 700 mi. (1,127 km)

Area: 290,586 sq. mi. (752,614 km²)

NATURE

Trees: Much of the land is a sparsely wooded savanna, whose trees are used mainly for firewood. Valuable forests of Rhodesian teak are found in the southwest. Teak grows in southwestern Zambia and is used in hardwood floors, furniture, and prefabricated housing. There also are pine and eucalyptus.

Animals: The grasslands support beef and dairy cattle, as well as elephants, hyenas, monkeys, leopards, antelopes, baboons, zebras, and hippopotamuses. There are several game parks. The largest reserve is at Luangwa Valley National Park, which is known for its herds of elephants.

Fish: Giant catfish, eel, and Nile perch are caught in Lake Kariba and Lake Tanganyika.

EVERYDAY LIFE

Food: Maize is the main food. It is the basis of *nshima*, a thick porridge, which is a staple of the Zambian diet.

Holidays:

January 1, New Year's Day
March, Good Friday
March, Holy Saturday
March 13, Zambia Youth Day
May 1, Labor Day
Fourth Tuesday in May, Africa Freedom Day
July 4, Heroes' Day
July 6, Unity Day
August 2, Farmers' Day
October 24, Independence Day
December 25, Christmas Day

Culture: The number of Zambian writers and artists is small. Wood carving, pottery, basket weaving, and house wall paintings are traditional Zambian arts. Music, dance, and songs are used in traditional rituals. Dancing is the most enduring aspect of African culture in Zambia. The construction of musical instruments is another form of artistic expression.

Western instruments have modified the Zambian music in the urban areas. Local dancers perform at the Open Air Museum at Livingstone, where there is a national museum, and a small museum on the Copperbelt, which displays artifacts of Central Africa.

Zambian people have many fables, riddles, proverbs, and creation myths as well as a strong tradition of oral history.

Sports and Recreation: Fishing is very popular at Lake Kariba, where many other water activities are enjoyed as well. Lake Tanganyika is another spot that is enjoyed by Zambians and tourists alike. Soccer, as in many countries of the world, is the favorite sport in Zambia. A national soccer team participated in the South Korean Olympics in 1988. A Zambian boxer won the bronze medal in the lightweight division in 1984.

Badminton, squash, baseball, and rugby are played also. Golf is expensive, as it is elsewhere, and it is considered a very prestigious sport. Girls enjoy netball (or basketball).

Communication: Before independence, European domination of the country's economic and cultural life was reflected in its press—all newspapers and periodicals were European enterprises. By the 1960s, however, new publications began printing news for Africans that reflected African interests and aspirations.

There are two daily newspapers and a number of provincial papers. The *Times of Zambia* is published in Ndola.

Radio has been an important medium. Radio Zambia is financed by government subsidies. News, public affairs, and musical programs are popular.

Television service was initiated in 1961. It is supported by government subsidy and by revenues from advertising and viewers' licenses. Imported programs come mostly from the United States or Great Britain.

Motion pictures are extremely popular. Films are used widely by various government bodies to promote public and community-development projects, such as farming, health, and sanitation.

Transportation: Two main railroad lines run from the Rhodesian border to the Copperbelt. The Tanzania-Zambia Railway Authority (TAZARA) line extends northeastward to the Tanzanian border and Dar es Salaam. The Benguela railroad runs from Angola's port city of Benguela into Zaire, and it has been the victim of the civil war that has raged in Angola for more than ten years. There are over 21,748 mi. (35,000 km) of roads. Government-owned Zambia Airways provides service to roughly twenty towns. Several international airlines fly to and from the airport at Lusaka.

Schools: After independence in 1964 there was a great expansion of the Zambia educational system. The government has attempted to establish universal free primary education (seven years), but a number of Zambians fail to continue beyond lower primary levels (five years), and relatively few go beyond lower secondary levels.

Zambia University, which opened in 1966, provides courses in humanities, social sciences, natural sciences, law, social work, business and public administration, and agriculture. The Zambia Institute of Technology, in Kitwe, offers technical courses, while the College of Applied Arts and Commerce focuses on commercial subjects.

Books in Zambia's schools are shockingly scarce.

Health: The government attempts to provide medical service at little or no cost in rural as well as urban areas. In the rapidly growing urban areas some private industries provide medical care for employees and dependents. Major medical problems include chronic illnesses such as malaria and malnutrition, as well as acute diseases such as measles, typhoid, dysentery, and river blindness. Only 4 percent of the people live beyond the age of sixty.

AIDS and alcoholism are also major health problems, and educational programs are being developed to deal with both.

Generally, Zambia suffers from a lack of trained medical personnel. Many turn to traditional medicine, such as herbal treatments.

ECONOMY AND INDUSTRY

Principal Products:
Agriculture: Cassava, peanuts, maize, millet, sorghum grain
Fishing: Perch and whitebait
Manufacturing and Processing: Flour, cement, copper products, wood products
Mining: Copper and cobalt

IMPORTANT DATES

4th to 6th Centuries A.D.—Bantu-speaking migrants come to area that is now Zambia from north, west, and south

6th Century—Region northwest of Victoria Falls is settled; Africans mine copper on the Copperbelt

1650—Lozi kingdom established on the Zambezi River

1851—Scottish missionary David Livingstone crosses the Zambezi River from the south; spends nearly twenty years exploring the region that will become Zambia

1878—Lewanika becomes king of the Lozi

1884-85—Berlin West Africa Conference, European powers settle claims on Africa; Britain and Portugal scramble to claim Zambian territory

1890—Lochner Treaty between Lozi king and the British South Africa Company headed by Cecil Rhodes

1905—Boundaries of "Northern Rhodesia" defined

1920s—Further discovery of copper brings rush of Europeans to the area

1924—British government takes over administration of Northern Rhodesia from Rhodes's British South Africa Company

1925—First "reserve" set up to contain Africans

1939—First junior secondary school for Africans opens

1948—First African political party formed (Northern Rhodesian African National Congress)

1953—Britain forms federation of Northern Rhodesia, Southern Rhodesia, and Nyasaland

1959—UNIP (United National Independence party) formed

1960—Kenneth Kaunda leads UNIP

1964—Northern Rhodesia becomes the independent nation Zambia

1969—President Kenneth Kaunda embarks on program of industrial and commercial nationalization

1973—Kenneth Kaunda cements one-party rule with new constitution

1980s—Zambia forms part of Front-Line States with liberating Africans in Namibia and South Africa

IMPORTANT PEOPLE

Simon Kapwepwe (1922-80), prominent political leader, politician of the opposition

Kenneth D. Kaunda (1924-   ), first president of the Republic of Zambia, 1964; reelected 1968, 1973, 1978, 1983

Lewanika (1842-1916), king of the Lozi; tried to maintain his people's independence

David Livingstone (1813-73), doctor and missionary; Scottish explorer of Zambezi River area; made his home in Zambia

John Mwanakatwe (1926-   ), first African minister of education

Harry Nkumbula (1916-   ), became president of Zambia African National Congress in 1951

Cecil Rhodes (1853-1902), British administrator and financier in South Africa; devoted himself to establishing Rhodesia as part of British empire

INDEX

Page numbers that appear in boldface type indicate illustrations

124

About the Author

Jason Lauré was born in Chehalis, Washington, and lived in California before joining the U.S. Army and serving in France. He attended Columbia University and worked for *The New York Times*.

He traveled to San Francisco and became a photographer during the turbulent 1960s. He recorded those events before setting out on the first of many trips to Africa. He covers the political life of that continent and has also made a number of expeditions across the Sahara.

Mr. Lauré has written about, and photographed in, forty countries in Africa. He has written three books, on South Africa, Portugal, and Bangladesh, in collaboration with Ettagale Blauer. Their Bangladesh book was nominated for a National Book Award. In the Enchantment of the World series, Mr. Lauré has written the book on Zimbabwe.

Mr. Lauré is married to Marisia Lauré, a translator.